Entrepreneur QUICK GUIDE

BUILDING, MARKETING, and SCALING

Your New Business

Entrepreneur Press, Publisher
Cover Design: Andrew Welyczko
Production and Composition: Nathaniel Roy

This publication is designed to provide accurate and authoritative information in regard to the subject matter covered. It is sold with the understanding that the publisher is not engaged in rendering legal, accounting, or other professional services. If legal advice or other expert assistance is required, the services of a competent professional person should be sought.

Library of Congress Cataloging-in-Publication Data
Names: Diamond, Stephanie, author. | Entrepreneur Media, The Staff of, author.
Title: Building, marketing, and scaling your new business / Stephanie Diamond, The Staff of Entrepreneur Media.
Description: Irvine : Entrepreneur Press, [2024] | Series: Entrepreneur quick guide | Includes index. | Summary: "Building, Marketing, and Scaling Your New Business will teach you how to establish an online presence, attract your ideal customers, and maximize your profits"-- Provided by publisher.
Identifiers: LCCN 2023044112 (print) | LCCN 2023044113 (ebook) | ISBN 9781642011739 (paperback) | ISBN 9781613084786 (epub)
Subjects: LCSH: New business enterprises. | Internet marketing. | Branding (Marketing) | Business planning.
Classification: LCC HD62.5 .D5154 2024 (print) | LCC HD62.5 (ebook) | DDC 658.1/1--dc23/eng/20240122
LC record available at https://lccn.loc.gov/2023044112
LC ebook record available at https://lccn.loc.gov/2023044113

BUILDING, MARKETING, and SCALING

Your New Business

1 Establish An Online Presence

2 Attract Your Ideal Customer

3 Maximize Your Profits

BY THE STAFF OF ENTREPRENEUR MEDIA AND STEPHANIE DIAMOND

CONTENTS

PART 3
SCALING

Introduction

ARE YOU PREPARED TO BUILD, MARKET, AND SCALE your new business? It can be a challenging and exciting journey that requires your full attention. With your purchase of the *Entrepreneur Quick Guide: Building, Marketing, and Scaling Your New Business*, you've taken a positive step toward making success happen.

Consider this book your essential toolkit designed to guide you through the early stages of growing your business. The information is broken down into manageable steps, so if this information is new to you, this guide will help you build a solid foundation.

Some of the topics covered include:

Building

Boosting your productivity with technology: Whether on the go or tethered to a desk, you can be more productive utilizing the latest technology. For example, you can hire a virtual assistant to assist with daily tasks and store content in the cloud for 24/7 access. Choose pared-down hardware and software tailored to your specific needs—no need to pay for pricey extras you won't use. With costs falling, you can get great deals on the basics.

Establishing your web presence: Building a website that promotes your business is critical to your success. You need to ensure that you have a well-designed site that's easy to navigate and has persuasive copy. Get the design, navigation, and compelling copy right from the beginning. Also, research before choosing a hosting platform, and don't hesitate to pursue certifications to establish customer trust and credibility.

Staying connected with technology: Keeping in touch using

technology such as broadband, Fios, and mobile devices contin-ues to drop in price. Choosing the right carrier and determining your data needs becomes an important decision. In addition, texting to stay connected in real-time has become a ubiquitous form of communication. There are many options and things to determine, like how often you travel and whether you have access to hotspots or choose to use prepaid phones. Choose what keeps you seamlessly connected and on budget.

Marketing

Focusing on brand-building: Consider how customers perceive you to create a solid brand. Project a consistent identity across touchpoints to stand out. Your primary goals are to set yourself apart, know your target customers, and project the personality you want them to remember you by. And make sure to leverage social proof—your advocates are your best asset.

Advertising and marketing your business: You should continu-ally focus your marketing plan on getting and keeping customers. That means you need to clearly understand where your company stands (called situational awareness) and how you will reach your marketing goals. Digital ads offer unmatched reach and analytics —make them your priority. Consider bringing in professionals for advertising, copywriting, and design to project a professional image. This will help you accelerate results.

Promoting your business: When deciding how to spread the word about your business, you'll need to think about creating a publicity plan. Advertising is good, but publicity generated by word of mouth and attention from the media is always more powerful. Schedule special events or stage a brick-and-mortar store grand opening to create excitement and kickstart buzz. You may feel a bit uncomfortable "tooting your own horn," but you're the one who must step up and make things happen. Perhaps you can co-sponsor an event or be part of a local contest or charity event. There are many ways of promoting your business; you just need to network and see what is happening in your community.

Selling techniques: As an entrepreneur, you may feel you are not equipped (or don't have the personality) to play a sales role, but you might be surprised by your expertise. As the creator, you are the expert on your product or service. Therefore, it's your job to lead the development of your 'unique selling proposition (USP). Your USP sets you apart from your competitors. You are just another faceless company trying to sell something without defining your USP. To nail it down, consider putting yourself in your customers' shoes and be clear about what motivates them to buy.

Providing excellent customer service: After you make the sale, you still have work to do. Repeat customers are the key to a successful ongoing business, so you must continue building customer relationships. You need to stay on top of new trends and listen to their comments. Determine how to surprise them with a discount or a free service. Also, make sure to motivate your staff to provide excellent service too.

Scaling

Tackling online advertising and marketing: Your website should serve as your prime asset. It gives you complete control over your messaging, branding, and content. The challenge is driving targeted traffic to your site due to the heavy volume of competitors. Search engines are your essential tool for solving this problem; optimizing for relevant keywords improves your visibility. Consider leveraging artificial intelligence and specialized tools like SEMrush or BuzzSumo to outperform your competition in search rankings. Additionally, don't overlook the power of local search to connect with your immediate community.

Spreading the word using online platforms: Social media platforms have become indispensable when building and sustaining a brand. A consistent content strategy, including blogging, is also crucial to your marketing. You can extend your reach by cross-promoting blog content on social platforms. In addition, establish your brand as a thought leader by strategically publishing expert articles on platforms frequented by your target audience.

Networking on social media: Businesses recognize the crucial role that social media plays in connecting with key business contacts. Platforms like LinkedIn are essential for connecting with two critical groups: (1) high-level networkers (HLNs) who are active and influential in their industries and (2) target market connections (TMCs) who are information seekers engaged in groups relevant to your business. Platforms like LinkedIn, Facebook, Instagram, and Twitter are foundational for initiating these connections. Remember that it's wise to keep your personal groups separate from your business groups when making connections.

Tips and Warnings: Many business resources and tip boxes (see examples below) are included in this book.

AHA!

Here you will find helpful information or ideas you may not have thought of before.

TIP

This box gives you ideas on how to do something better or more efficiently, or simply how to work smarter.

WARNING

Here we remind you to heed the warnings to avoid common mistakes and pitfalls that others have made before you.

FYI
This box points you to current and often comprehensive websites that you might seek out for business information.

SAVE
Look for this box to provide valuable tips on ways you can save money during startup.

Entrepreneur Quick Guide: Building, Marketing and Scaling Your New Business is a timely and essential book for committed entrepreneurs like you. It addresses the genuine joys and challenges of business ownership.

Use its guidance as your road map to success, and make sure to enjoy your exciting business adventure!

PART 1
Building

CHAPTER 1 BUSINESS 24/7
USING TECHNOLOGY TO BOOST YOUR PRODUCTIVITY

CHAPTER 2 YOUR ALL-IMPORTANT WEBSITE
BUILDING YOUR WEB PRESENCE

CHAPTER 3 KEEP IN TOUCH
USING TECHNOLOGY TO STAY CONNECTED

CHAPTER 1
Business 24/7

Using Technology to Boost Your Productivity

IF YOU'RE LIKE MOST BUSINESSPEOPLE, you probably have a main base of operations you call your "office," "home base," or "headquarters." It could be a retail store, a factory floor, or a trailer on a construction site. It could also be a room in your home or a cubicle within a larger office complex. It is where you can usually be found 9 to 5 or whatever your typical office hours might be.

These days, thanks to mobile technology, your exact location could vary widely. Nowadays, entrepreneurs and employees alike are just as likely to be found working from home, at a client's office, from a hotel room, at the airport, at a Starbucks, or while traveling on board an airplane or train. Widespread use of devices such as smartphones, tablets, and laptops means your office can be virtually anywhere, and you can stay connected to your co-workers, clients, and customers anywhere, anytime. Cloud computing has also allowed data to be stored remotely, in the cloud, and be accessed from any of your devices, from anywhere at any time.

Business that's conducted away from the traditional office goes by a lot of names, such as mobile working or telecommuting—the latter term underlining the importance of telecommunications in enabling this activity. Another way to think about it is that, in reality, the office is you—or, at the very least, it becomes whatever work space you happen to be occupying at the moment.

Work is now something you do rather than a place you go to.

Today, most businesses have moved far away from desktop computers and landline phones. Internet connectivity, powerful mobile versions of office tools, smartphones, and wireless tablets have changed the face of business technology, making the physical location for many businesses (other than restaurants and retail businesses) less significant than ever before.

Many entrepreneurs have the equivalent of fully equipped virtual offices in the laptops, smartphones, tablets, and other devices they carry around. Some enterprises have even become virtual companies with employees spending most of their time at separate locations and meeting only occasionally, often via Zoom, or some other online meeting provider. Basically, you're "in the office" whenever you're telecommuting.

The goal isn't always to do away with the traditional office; it's to use networking and communications technologies to create your "extended office." Your extended office isn't a real, physical location; it's virtual just like the internet.

People have been teleworking for decades, but our current degree of mobility is a direct outgrowth of the internet and the mobile devices that allow us to easily connect to the internet from anywhere.

Virtually on the Road

Thanks to the latest technology, there's a wide range of products and online services to help you become more productive. The Apple iPhone and iPad, for example, offer thousands of business-oriented applications that allow users to truly customize their phones and transform them into the ultimate time management, contact management, and personal productivity tools.

For the on-the-go entrepreneur, the trick is to choose technology-based tools, whether it's an iPhone, iPad, Samsung Galaxy, Microsoft Surface, Chromebook, netbook, or laptop, that best fits your work habits and style, and that you're most comfortable using.

After all, you want to boost your productivity—not drown yourself in technology that's not appropriate or overly complicated for what you need it to do.

Equipping Your Virtual Office

Even though you may be starting your first business, you're probably fairly experienced with desktops and/or laptops, tablets, and smartphones as well as other productivity equipment needed to get your enterprise off the ground.

One unfailing characteristic of consumer and small-business technologies is that each new iteration delivers more for less. Depending on how much mobility you need, you may find yourself buying more individual pieces of equipment than in years past, but the price tag on each one is typically lower than last year and the year before that. It's not that they're shoddy—quite the contrary. But their resale values are continuously being undercut by cheaper and more powerful successors.

Need an Assistant? Go Virtual

There's a lot of busy work that comes with being an entrepreneur—or an executive of any kind. But are you making the most of your time doing a lot of this work? Not always. That's where a virtual assistant can help. A virtual assistant can be a great first "employee" for your business—one you needn't hire full time unless necessary.

Hiring a virtual assistant will give you a chance to see the real challenges of task delegation and a glimpse into managing people. Make sure you have a clear list of tasks you will delegate—and communicate exactly what you want done. This can take some time to get right, but in the end, you'll free yourself from time-wasting tasks.

You should hire a virtual assistant when you realize you will soon be overwhelmed by your workload and can't move forward without some help.

Here are several tasks that are perfectly suited for virtual assistants:

- **SEO and social media.** An assistant can research trending topics, keep on top of popular keywords related to your business, do research for your site's content, help make sure you are aware of trends, create and maintain a social media calendar for postings, and even suggest social media content (and tweaks as you go) to help make your social presence stronger.
- **Repeatable or template tasks.** Repeatable tasks are those items on your to-do list that keep popping up week after week. These tasks follow the same process each time, which means that a little training can empower a virtual assistant to successfully complete these tasks and make more time for growing the business.
- **Creative, but time-consuming.** Other tasks for the right virtual assistant could include blog posting, creating simple workbooks and materials for clients, and developing email templates for future use.

Before you hire a virtual assistant, track your time for a few weeks and notice how much time you spend on each task. Then find the average time that each task takes. Next, make a list of the most time-consuming tasks, that will not require a lot of detailed training and create a specific virtual assistant job description. Include the tools, apps, and software that you are planning to use. And to make training easier, use screen capture technology to record yourself completing a task from start to finish—to be shared with your new assistant.

FYI—when it comes to financial tasks, do them yourself or leave them for the bookkeeper or accountant. You can't risk handing over such tasks, or those with personal information, to a virtual assistant.

Therefore, you should think about office tools and technology slightly differently than you do other durables. Here are a few truisms to consider when buying hardware (although they don't necessarily apply to software):

- Even the most expensive office item—the desktop or laptop computer—is dirt cheap by historical measures.
- Whatever you buy and whenever you buy it, it will appear expensive and underpowered compared to succeeding versions. New computer technology is available every three to six months. The computer you purchase brand-new today will be outdated by more powerful equipment within months and will probably need to be replaced altogether within two to three years if you want to stay current.
- Theoretically, office equipment pays for itself in a short period by enhancing your productivity; it then helps you make money by letting you do whatever you do faster and better.

Treat your current technology-related purchases as a simple business expense rather than investment in capital equipment it actually is. Irrespective of how you treat these items on your tax return, don't try to extract the value of this equipment over years. Yes, the products will work just fine and continue to deliver productivity for years. But their costs are likely recovered within weeks or months—no depreciation calculations required.

That's not to say you shouldn't get the best buy you can. Cash is always precious. But so is your time, and price tags are usually overshadowed by the return on investment from most office products. The real issue when shopping for office equipment is whether the new machine will deliver a higher rate of productivity than the old. It's a mistake to try to squeeze the last bit of usefulness out of older equipment when an update could result in higher levels of moneymaking. Conversely, don't buy new products just because they have more bells and whistles. If your cell phone serves your purposes, hang onto it longer. If your computer meets your needs and the software is sufficient for your business, don't spend more just because there's a new model available. Remember, you don't have to keep up with the Joneses unless they are competing for your business. Each time you get new equipment, there's a learning curve that can slow you or your employees down. New versions of products are great if they benefit your business, but not necessary if they don't.

TIP

While computers and mobile devices run using a wide range of different operating systems, most are designed to operate seamlessly in a work environment. So if you're using an Apple MacBook Pro laptop, for example, you'll have no trouble transferring data and files with co-workers or clients using Windows-based computers. You can run Windows-based software on the latest Macs, and Microsoft Word for iPad has gone a long way in making the iPad a virtual office, too. There are also multiple apps created for easy storage and transfer of documents between operating systems.

Being Well-Connected

The first concern when equipping yourself and your office (virtual or otherwise) is connectivity. You have an expanding constellation of stuff, and it's more important than ever that it all works together for maximum effect. Efficiency today means being well-connected—both inside and outside the walls of your company.

Even if you start as a solo operator working from a home office, you'll want to connect electronically to clients and suppliers and possibly share proposals, spreadsheets, and other data files. This not only requires a phone and texting but usually some level of compatibility among productivity software and wireless devices. That used to mean sticking with only the most popular operating systems and applications for seamless data transfer among employees and business partners.

SAVE

Depending on your needs, you might not need to invest $1,500 to $2,500 for a state-of-the-art laptop. If your main tasks when traveling include surfing the web, word processing, and spreadsheet management, for example, a less cumbersome, smaller, and lightweight netbook may work for you just fine. The latest netbooks cost only around $350. Or you might find that a tablet, like an iPad, Microsoft Surface, or Samsung Galaxy is all you need for the office. Those run between $400 and $1,200.

Today, however, PCs can usually communicate more easily with Macs, Androids, and iPhones; in fact, any peripheral that connects to a computer via a USB connection will most likely work with all computers on a network. Sure, you may still encounter minor compatibility issues, but for the most part, exchanging data and files is easier than ever regardless of what types of computer equipment are being used.

What's more, Google's rise in the shared document space has been tremendous. It's easy to selectively share—and set parameters around who can edit and who can simply view—spreadsheets, Word documents, PowerPoint presentations, and many other kinds of documents through Google Drive. Many large companies even use Gmail's business services. Free or low-cost services like Dropbox, WeTransfer, and Box.com have also made it possible to skip the USB and thumb drives altogether by acting as a transfer and file storage and collaboration service—with the added element of tight security for transferring and storing files.

At your office, it's the network that helps you coordinate your tools—both those inside the office and out—and share them and the data on them among co-workers and partners. Networks include your local area network, Bluetooth connections between devices, cellular connections over a wide area, and of course, the ultimate backbone: the internet. Increasingly, these files and connections can all be backed up to "the cloud."

It's not really our portable devices—laptop computers, smartphones, netbooks, and tablets—that extend our office. It's this infrastructure that connects all our devices together and provides quick and easy access to shared information, both in-house and outside, via global network providers.

The Cloud and You

Simply put, the cloud means applications and services that people access via the internet instead of installing software on their computers. If you're online, you're somewhere in the cloud. If you use Facebook, Gmail, or Twitter, you're using the cloud. "Many valuable services that once required installing applications have become available as cloud services," explains Mikal Belicove, a market positioning, social media, and management consultant specializing in website usability and business blogging. Often, businesses can use free versions of these applications in the cloud, while full-featured versions are available at low subscription rates.

"The cloud is more heavy-duty and provides more utility than initially perceived," says Belicove. You can access customer relationship management tools like those offered by Salesforce.com but also project management applications and many other types of helpful programs and utilities. In fact, most applications and functions, from email to Google Docs and more, are cloud-based or stored in "the cloud." The upside: access when and where you need it (not just from your desktop or laptop). For some business owners, this means you can operate your entire office—from bookkeeping to files—from the cloud.

Cloud storage is popular these days, because it can be cheaper, offers data tiering (meaning you can quickly retrieve files you may need more often), and stores multiple copies of your data, but there are some downsides. For example, by working remotely you will be without the benefit of your usual, faster internet service, and may not be able to access your files. Retrieval can also be slow at times and security is still questionable in some instances.

It Takes Two

Even if you're starting as a sole proprietor, you should have at least two connected computers. It doesn't have to be two desktop computers. If you travel a lot, one could be a laptop or tablet.

It's only a matter of time before your hard drive crashes, you get a virus, or there's some inscrutable problem with the first PC's on/off button—whatever. Computers are durable, but all equipment can fail, and when it does it's very unpleasant.

What will you do if the machine holding your critical business information happens to be among the 100,000 computers that lightning strikes every year? Even if you're among that fraction of users who have their data backed up somewhere, how long will it take for you to run out and buy a new computer and add all your usual software configured the way you like it so that data can be read? How many hours or days can your business be offline from customers and business partners?

TIP

Remote backup services, such as Carbonite.com, and extremely low-cost, high-capacity external hard drives make it easy and inexpensive to automatically and continuously back up your data. Now you have no excuse for not properly backing up your data. So if something happens to your primary computer, you can be up and running, without losing any data, within minutes or hours—not days or weeks. To check out alternative back-up programs check out Capterra: capterra.com/p/223152/Carbonite/alternatives/.

Realistically, you need at least one duplicate of your main computer that you can turn to without losing a step. That could be a thumb drive, printed hard copies, or an external hard drive that keeps data safe and off your computer or the internet. For some businesses, cloud storage is enough to make a second backup computer or external hard drive unnecessary. But be aware: The cloud isn't infallible. Some services have experienced outages that can last an hour or two—or up to 12 hours.

Serving It Up

Ultimately, you want to build a virtual network that ties your office and its equipment to all those other places and devices you use for work. Thanks to wireless networking, your home, back deck, a local coffee shop, the park, or even your car, van, or RV can be part of your extended office.

But the most logical place to start is by connecting your main computer and its backup. Your primary workstation will likely become the heart of your operation, where you generate spreadsheets, keep your books, create sales presentations, browse the web, and do your word processing. If you run a one-person operation, that's usually where the master copy of everything is kept—and, if you have help, no one but you should have full access to its data.

Again, even if you're a one-person operation, you need another computer mirroring that system (or a reliable data backup solution). As your company grows, you might find it cheaper and more convenient to keep master copies of software and even data on a central computer and give different workstations access to more or less of it, depending on the needs of individual employees.

SAVE

If you're looking to create a network and link multiple computers and peripherals within your home office, many computer retailers will help you set this up for free (or for a small fee) when you purchase equipment from them. When shopping for computer equipment, ask what support services are available directly from the retailer.

Computer Networking

The traditional way to create your LAN (local area network) is to string inexpensive Category 5 cable between the Ethernet adapters of two or more computers. You may need to buy a small and inexpensive Ethernet card to plug into one or more of your computers, if any of them are old. Most computers today come with built-in Ethernet adapters.

Easier still is to network your computers wirelessly using wifi network adapters. These come in a variety of network speeds and adapter styles—Ethernet or USB ports or as an add-in card—for connecting computers. Wifi transceivers are hugely popular, a standard feature of laptops, and available in all smartphones and tablets. More U.S. households now use wifi wireless technology for home networking than cabled Ethernet. Wifi technology is built into most printers sold today as well. Wifi is now widely available at little-to-no cost in airports, hotels, coffee shops, and other public places, and it delivers this connectivity on the road. But exercise caution here: Your connection in these public places is not always as secure as you would like. To keep your data private, avoid doing bank transactions or work on highly sensitive materials in such locations.

Most smartphones can be set up with wifi hotspot capabilities for a small, additional monthly fee on your wireless plan. Some plans, like unlimited data plans from Verizon Wireless, T-Mobile, or AT&T, include the hotspot capability so you can always use your phone as a wifi connection for your laptop, tablet, or other wifi-capable device while you're on the road.

Broadband data channels on cellular networks provide much wider connectivity. Cell phone networks are increasingly able to transfer data at lightning-fast speeds. Besides cell phones, this technology works with tablets, netbooks, and laptops—making the net available anywhere regardless of whether there's a nearby electrical outlet or wifi hotspot.

It's Now or Never

In most cases, you'll probably find it more advantageous—and certainly more convenient—to expense, rather than depreciate, computer and telecommunications equipment on your tax returns. That way, there's less paperwork and no mind-bending depreciation calculations that change every year. Also, the time value of money tells us that a lump-sum refund to you today is always worth more than pro-rata shares over the next three to five years.

Uncle Sam has been cooperating in recent years by raising the amount of business equipment you can expense rather than depreciate. No, he isn't getting soft and generous. Why then? Adam Smith, the father of modern economics, said it first: New equipment generates new, higher levels of productivity, which generates increased profits, which generates increased taxes. Speak with your accountant about the latest tax deductions and allowances available.

Choosing Office Equipment

There are two things on which you can rely these days when buying just about any piece of office equipment:

1. The minimum configuration is going to support 95 percent (or more) of what you want to do.
2. Prices will be so low as to eliminate just about all chance of buyer's remorse.

Add to that the ease with which internet shopping sites let you comparison shop, and you have a confluence of factors that make it pretty hard to go wrong when buying office equipment. Computers and peripherals are constantly evolving, but the choice of models and features are broad and deep.

When it comes to PCs, you can choose from dozens of well-known manufacturers, such as Dell, HP, or Lenovo, all of which run the Windows operating system.

Apple offers greater ease of use, the availability of Apple retail stores nationwide, and a sleeker design than most PCs, but they're also typically quite a bit more expensive and offer less software options. On that note, there is no one "right" computer brand, printer type, phone system, or fax solution for everyone, any more than everyone needs the same model Chevy or Ford. You're unique, and your business probably is, too. Your enterprise will have its own unique set of equipment needs that probably differ from those of the business next door. Not a problem. Web shopping sites let you quickly find just what you need.

Buying Business Class

Your goal when purchasing computer equipment should be to select items that not only meet all your computing needs today, but will also grow with you over the next two to three years until your next upgrade. Buy more than you need now so you'll be able to continue to run the latest versions of the software and applications you need to properly manage your business.

You'll want a business-class, rather than a first-class, computer. That means instead of going for the cutting-edge graphics and processor speeds preferred by enthusiasts of multimedia entertainment, gaming, and other photographic activities, a business user's money is better spent getting just a little more of all the standard stuff—memory, storage, a higher resolution or larger display—those things that not only make computing more pleasing, but also enhance your productivity. Of course, all of this is predicated on the type of business you are running.

Better computers, with more memory and faster processing speeds, can help with things like waiting for databases to update, web pages to download, and insufficient memory errors. You'll want to get the best business productivity enhancer you can afford.

SAVE

How long will a computer last? To maximize your return on investment, replace it every three to four years, according to conventional practices. Older computers negatively impact security and productivity, and cost considerably more per year to support and maintain—often twice the cost of newer technology.

Take Note

When it comes to laptops, focus on their computing power (processor speed, memory, hard-drive capacity, available ports, DVD/CD drive if needed, etc.) and battery life as well as the overall size and weight of the unit. A laptop that weighs five pounds or less is a lot easier to lug around when you're traveling than a larger laptop that weighs six to eight pounds.

However, if your laptop computer will be your primary computer, and you'll need serious computing power while on the go, you may want to spend more for a unit with a larger display and extra computing muscle. On the flip side, if you're looking for a small "backup" computer, you'll want one that is lightweight. You can typically get a netbook, which might be the perfect solution.

A typical laptop will generally run a few hundred dollars less than an equivalent desktop model, and name-brand laptops can easily be found for as little as $500. Laptops suitable for serious business users typically cost $700 to $1,600.

Some of the big-box stores offer computer repair service plans. But read the contract carefully; often such plans are very specific in what they cover and leave out a lot of things. In some cases, they also take on more than they can service in a reasonable amount of time and you're left waiting for them to get around to fixing your computer. For that reason, you're better off finding local computer repair services that understand the problem and give you a reasonable cost and time frame to make the necessary repairs. Smaller businesses also offer the opportunity to work with the same person or a few people on a regular basis so that when you have computer issues, they have an idea of what your difficulties might be. It's like having a good mechanic who knows your car rather than having to deal with someone new every time you have a problem.

The Well-Dressed Computer

The minimum you should look for in terms of technical specifications for a desktop or laptop changes constantly. As a general rule, look for a computer with a fast processing speed, a sizable amount of Random Access Memory (RAM), and a large-capacity hard drive. You also want to think about the screen size, resolution, and graphics card. Depending on your needs, a touch screen can make life easier if you'd like to get a break from having your fingers on the keyboard all the time.

Office Productivity Software

A computer is useless without the right software to support your business activities. The most popular suite of business-related applications is, without a doubt, Microsoft Office. It's available for both PCs and Macs. There are, however, other business application suites that also offer word processing, spreadsheet, database management, scheduling, contact management, and presentation tools.

One of these software suites alone could cost $150 to $400 or more, depending on the components included. Computers are so cheap that not many computer manufacturers include an office suite on a standard hard drive, but most will offer Microsoft Office pre-installed as an upgrade.

In addition, a host of competitors have built business-friendly products that might work just as well for you—and they're mostly free. Google has the most popular option, with its suite of Google Sheets (for online spreadsheets), Google Slides (for collaborative presentations), Google Docs (for creating collaborative documents), and more (including a forms library that is robust enough to meet the needs of almost any business). Because the programs are cloud-based, you don't need to download software and you can access files from anywhere at any time. Other popular free applications include LibreOffice (libreoffice.org), Dropbox Paper (dropbox.com/paper), and Apple iWork (apple.com/iwork), which is for iOS operating systems—or for any systems via the cloud.

Two other kinds of software you need are a security suite and accounting program. You'll want an all-encompassing security suite, such as those offered by companies like Norton (us. norton.com); Bitdefender (bitdefender.com); Broadcom, which now offers products by Symantec (broadcom.com); Trend Micro (trendmicro.com); McAfee (mcafee.com); and Panda (pandasecurity.com/usa). These applications include a firewall, regularly updated antivirus and anti-spyware definitions, email scanning, and other protections for $50 to $140 per year. If you're running Mac computers, different types of security software may be needed, depending on how you'll be using the computer. You can check out rankings, ratings, and articles on the latest versions of security software at *PC Magazine* (pcmag.com). Don't skimp on buying what you need to keep your computer as safe as possible.

Whether you use an accounting professional, you also need a good basic accounting program from a company like Intuit (intuit. com), Sage (sage.com), or Microsoft (microsoft.com) to keep up with your checkbooks, bank accounts, invoices, bills, taxes, and inventory. Most of these programs let you pay bills and download bank account information electronically, use your printer to create checks, and link to tax preparation software so you can minimize your tax liability. Some popular programs are Intuit's QuickBooks Pro, Bookkeeper, and Sage 50cloud Accounting.

Say No to Cash Flow Shortcuts

Got a cash-flow problem? Who doesn't? Don't solve it by succumbing to the gazillion counterfeit software offers filling your email inbox. If you get caught purchasing these low-cost knockoffs, you'll be fined heavily and could face criminal charges.

Instead look into using open-source software, which is often just as powerful as the higher-priced commercial software, only it's 100 percent free. SourceForge (sourceforge.net) is an excellent resource for finding and downloading a wide range of open-source software for any operating system.

However, if you use one of these programs, it's important you keep in mind that free doesn't always equate with safe. Blogger Patricia Johnson wrote in a blog post for WhiteSourceSoftware.com that "Open-source security vulnerabilities are an extremely lucrative opportunity for hackers." She added, "Open-source software presents legal, engineering, and security challenges, and when organizations aren't on top of the quality of open-source components they are using, they could unknowingly be incorporating vulnerable, risky, unlicensed, and out-of-date components."

Peripherals

There are any number of things you can add to your computer these days—or wirelessly connect to your office network. Most popular besides printers are speakers, a webcam, external hard drive, headphones, a wireless keyboard, or a second monitor. If you have an iPhone or Android, you can also connect these devices to your computer to sync data.

Many businesses need at least one good-quality laser printer; however, if your printing needs involve color or photo-quality output, an inkjet or high-end photo printer will also be useful. When choosing printers, look at the unit's resolution, print speed, and paper-tray size.

For most small businesses, an all-in-one device (sometimes

referred to as a multifunction device, or MFD) that includes a printer, scanner, fax machine, and copier is ideal. Plus, you may want to invest in an external hard drive to back up important data; otherwise, invest in a cloud-based system like Carbonite to back up data.

Most peripherals these days connect to a computer via Fire-Wire, USB, or Bluetooth wireless connection. It's common for a desktop computer to have up to ten or more devices and peripherals connected to it, all of which work seamlessly with your software.

As a general rule, focus first on your needs, then shop around for the most advanced technology you can afford. If you don't need a color laser printer, for example, opt for a less expensive black-and-white laser printer with a faster print speed and larger paper tray. Or if you're choosing between laser printers and inkjet printers, consider not only the cost of the hardware (the printer itself), but also the ongoing cost of toner or ink cartridges as well as the printer's speed. If you'll frequently be producing 100-page reports, a printer that churns out 15 to 30 pages per minute is much more useful than one that prints just 8 pages per minute with a feeder that holds only 25 sheets.

Once you determine your needs, shopping for computer peripherals online will typically save you time and money. Reserve a visit to the local consumer electronics or office supply superstore to see and touch the latest technology firsthand before making your purchases.

MFDs are priced between $100 and $800 for small businesses or several thousand dollars for larger companies with significant needs. You can get an MFD that packs an incredible amount of functionality from any of the well-known companies, such as HP, Canon, Brother, Epson, and Kyocera.

FYI

If your daily printing needs are limited and you primarily only print large single-order materials (like brochures, business cards, checks, etc.), consider an online printing service like Vistaprint (www.vistaprint.com).

In some cases, it might be useful to think of these categories of peripherals as supplies, rather than equipment, because the replacement toner cartridges for MFDs and individual copiers and printers can cost as much as the hardware itself. Your MFD choice will also depend on what you need. If you only need a printer, you don't need an MFD and can scan that occasional copy with your iPhone. Keep in mind that the one big drawback to an MFD is that if something goes wrong with the machine, you are not only out one function but multiple functions.

Suffice to say, entrepreneurship is no longer a stationary activity. Entrepreneurs go where the action is, stay productive en route, and use technology to adapt to changing market conditions and ad hoc business needs. With today's technology, you can make the most of what is available wherever you are.

CHAPTER 2

Your All-Important Website

Building Your Web Presence

WHY PUT YOUR BUSINESS ONLINE? The answer is simple. In today's business world, it's essential that your business have an online presence if you want to stay competitive. Your prospective and existing customers use the internet for a wide range of purposes, such as researching products they need, then purchasing those items from the comfort of their homes, offices, or anywhere else they may be. Unless you're running a very small local business, you won't be taken seriously without a web presence.

Sounds Like a Plan

If you plan to sell anything online, having an ecommerce plan is as important as your original business plan.

The first step in writing an ebusiness plan is to decide what kind of experience you want your online customers to have. And that starts with website goals. Who are your target customers? What do they need? Are they getting information only or can they buy products from your site? These key questions, asked and answered early on, will determine how much time and money you'll need to develop and maintain an online presence.

Second, decide what products or services you will offer. How will you position and display them? Will you offer both online and offline purchasing? How will you handle shipping and returns?

Additionally, don't overlook the need for customer service—consider creating chatbots to answer customer questions 24/7 without requiring a live person to be available. (If it's appropriate for the type of business you have, a toll-free phone number should be prominently displayed that customers can call at designated times to get their questions answered.)

As you explore the web for vendors to support your ebusiness, have a clear idea of how you want to handle the "back end" of the business. If you decide to sell online, you'll need a shopping cart component, which is a means of handling credit card processing, and an organized order fulfillment process. However, you may decide that your site is informational only, and you will continue to process transactions offline.

Steps to a Successful Web Business

More and more businesses are launching as online-only ventures because that's where an ever-increasing number of customers are shopping. If you expect to get much of your revenue through your website, according to Allen Moon, founder of On Deck Marketing, you'll need to consider these seven steps for successful ecommerce businesses:

1. Find a need and fill it. Look for a market first, not a product. If your business will be primarily online, look to online forums and social media to figure out the problem you're solving and how to best position it.
2. Write copy that sells. Find compelling and enticing ways to draw people in. Create urgency and appeal to bring people through the sales process.
3. Design and build an easy-to-use (user-friendly) website. If it's not simple, expect potential customers to abandon their purchase before they hit "buy." Don't go overboard with fancy interfaces that take too long to load or complex purchase systems to pay.

4. Use search engines to drive traffic to your site. Consider pay-per-click style advertising to start.
5. Establish an expert reputation for yourself. Give away free expert content. Write blogs or articles, post photos and videos, or any other content that people will find useful. Distribute that content through social media sites like Facebook, Instagram, or LinkedIn—and link to other websites like those of your local chamber of commerce or Rotary Club.
6. Follow up with your customers and subscribers via email. Build an opt-in list so you can email customers with new products and offers.
7. Increase your income through back-end sales and upselling. At least 36 percent of people who have purchased from you once will buy from you again if you follow up with them. Offer them products and services that complement their original purchase. Also entice them with discounts, specials, and online content that touts what they see and why they should buy from you.

The internet changes so fast that one year online equals about five years in the real world. But the principles of how to start and grow a successful online business haven't changed much.

Finally, even if you build an amazing website, don't assume people will find you on their own. If you simply build it, they will not come. If you want to develop a consistent flow of traffic to your site, it's essential that you plan, execute, and maintain an ongoing and multifaceted promotional strategy that's carefully targeted to your audience. This is in addition to the promotions, advertising, and marketing you already do if you also have a brick-and-mortar business.

"The website should be viewed as an integral part of the marketing effort—as another 'front door,' if you will, into the business," says Frank Catalano, a marketing strategy consultant. "After all, the site is a way to distribute information, gather customer feedback, and even sell a product or service. Just promoting a website without regard to overall business goals and other marketing efforts is pointless."

TIP

Building and maintaining a well-designed online presence, particularly a website with an ecommerce component, requires a significant time and financial commitment. For more details on how to accomplish this successfully and professionally without spending a fortune, pick up a copy of *The Digital Marketing Handbook: A Step-by-Step Guide to Creating Websites That Sell* (Entrepreneur Press, 2018) by Robert W. Bly.

The Name Game

One of your first "to do" items is to make a list of possible website names or URLs. This is typically the name of your business with .com or, perhaps, .net at the end. Search for the name you've chosen on various search engines to see if it is already being used. If you haven't launched your business, you can alter the business name to meet what is available online. In fact, most new business owners come up with the name of their business in conjunction with the .com address they will use online.

Then run, don't walk, to your computer, go to your favorite search engine, and type in "domain registration." You will find a list of companies, such as NetworkSolutions.com, Bluehost. com, GoDaddy.com, Hostgator.com, or Register.com, that will guide you through the simple domain registration process. For a modest fee, you can register a domain name for one or more years. Most of the well-known sites won't steer you wrong.

If the name you decide on is taken, you'll want to have at least two or three backup options. Let's say that you sell flowers, and you would like to register your online name as flowers.com.

A search shows that flowers.com is taken. Your second choice is buyflowers.com, but that's spoken for as well. Many of the domain name registrars, like GoDaddy.com or Register.com, offer several alternatives that are still available.

From the available names, choose one that's easy to spell and remember, and describes what your company does. Make sure, however, you're not imposing on someone else's trademark or copyrighted name.

If you choose a domain name that's difficult to spell or that might easily be confused with something else, also register the most common misspellings, or what you think people might accidentally type into their browser to find your website. For example, Google.com also owns Gogle.com. If you don't do this, your competition might, and they could wind up stealing some of your website traffic.

SAVE

Many domain registration services offer additional free or low-cost options. Domain parking, which holds your registered domain name at no charge until you're ready to launch, is one example. Email forwarding allows you to use your new domain name to receive email, while domain forwarding directs traffic to an existing site or web page. You can also save money if you preregister your domain name for multiple years.

Once you've chosen a name, prompts on the domain registration site will guide you through a simple registration procedure. You'll generally be offered a one-, two-, or three-year registration package. Once you pick a domain name and start promoting it, you'll want to stick with it. Otherwise, you'll confuse your customers and could lose web traffic. Some business owners have several domain names linking to the same website. These different domain names can be used as part of separate marketing and promotional plans that target an audience or lead to specific pages that generate many views.

Why is domain name registration imperative? Everyone wants a catchy name, so registering yours ensures that no one else can use it as long as you maintain your registration. For a small investment, you can hold your place on the internet until you're ready to launch.

With your ecommerce name established, start telling people your domain name and promoting it heavily. Make sure you've done everything you can do offline to tell people about your site at the same time you actually go online. Print your web address on your business cards, brochures, letterhead, invoices, and press releases as well as on your product packaging and within product user manuals and advertisements. Stick it on other items, too, such as mouse pads, T-shirts, promotional key chains, and your company's vehicles.

Website Basics

Once you've registered your domain name and have a plan in place for what you want to offer prospective and existing customers online, the next major challenge is designing and building your website or online presence.

What makes a good website? Before getting enmeshed in design details, get the big picture by writing a site outline. In addition to basic text, your website can incorporate photos, illustrations, animation, videos, audio clips, music, and a plethora of other multimedia elements or content that will convey information to your target audience in an easy-to-understand, visually appealing, and appropriate manner. However, the content you develop and publish should directly relate to and help you achieve the goals and objectives you've set for your website.

A well-thought-out site outline includes:

- *Content*. The key to a successful site is good content. Let visitors know what you have to offer, who you are (in an "About Us" section), and why they should buy from you. Provide product information incentives to buy and return again, and ways to contact you. A blog can bring back visitors to read about your expertise in the field of your business.

Once your site is up and running, continually update and add fresh content to keep people coming back. But don't overwhelm them with too many things to read or look at. Overly busy sites tend to turn people off. Clean design and easy-to-read content are key. Sometimes less is more. Research many other sites to see what layouts you like.

- *Structure.* Decide how many pages to have and how they'll be linked to each other. Choose graphics and icons that enhance the content. Overly goofy icons and imagery can be a turnoff if you want your business to portray a professional feel. Conversely, if fun and ease-of-use is a selling point for your company, images that are too posed or too professional may not match your persona.

- *Design.* With the content and structure in place, site design comes next. Whether you're using an outside designer or doing it yourself, concentrate on simplicity, readability, and consistency. Avoid gimmicks and too many bells and whistles. Remember to focus on what you want to accomplish.

- *Navigation.* Make it easy and enjoyable for visitors to browse the site. For example, use no more than two or three links to major areas, and never leave visitors at a dead end.

- *Credibility.* This is an issue that shouldn't be lost in the bells and whistles of establishing a website. Your site should reach out to every visitor, letting them know why they should buy your product or service. It should look very professional, match the persona you want to convey, and give potential customers the same feeling of confidence they would get with a phone call or face-to-face visit with you. If you have a physical presence, remind visitors that you don't exist only in cyberspace. Your company's full contact information—company name, address, telephone, and email—should appear on all or most of your individual web pages and be displayed prominently on your site's homepage.

- *Review everything.* Before you launch your site, make sure you proofread it carefully for spelling and grammar. This sounds obvious, but it's hard to believe how many websites are out there with misspelled words and poor grammar. Also, make sure links to your pages or to other websites (such as those of businesses that are complementary to yours) are all working. And since so many people are using their mobile devices to search, make sure your layout and design look good on smaller screens, such as cell phones and tablets. Remember, while you may be creating the content on a large 17-inch screen, potential customers may be reading it on their smartphones.

Start with an outline, which will help you get the most out of your website design/ecommerce budget. It will also help you determine whether you, or someone in your company, can design portions of the website or if you need to solicit outside help. That way, when you hire someone, it will only be for the parts of the job that you'll need to have outsourced. Again, it's important to look at many other sites and see what you like about their layout, design, and overall appearance.

At this point, you have two options: You can bring your detailed outline, plus your list of websites with designs and layouts that you like, to a prospective web designer, a freelancer, or you can go the do-it-yourself route. Once a designer has your outline, the process will be more efficient, but creating a website from scratch can still be costly and time-consuming. Consider researching one of the many website or ecommerce turnkey solution services, which allow you to design, publish, and manage a website or ecommerce site by customizing website templates using online design and management tools. These services are inexpensive, powerful, and allow you to create highly professional websites with no programming skills.

There are a few possible reasons why you'd want to hire a website designer and/or programmer to have your site created from scratch vs. using a turnkey solution. One reason would be if you absolutely require specialized functionality (either on the front or back end of the site) that isn't offered by the turnkey solutions. You might also feel uncomfortable using a turnkey solution or feel you need to stand out from competitors in a way those solutions don't allow. Be cautious: Many startups initially spend too much on a custom-designed site and regret the decision because their financial resources could have been put to better use elsewhere.

SAVE

You don't need an expensive website designer—or any designer in many cases. Squarespace has become a go-to for many small and new businesses. It is a one-stop solution for creating a website and can provide quite a few extras, like ecommerce, hosting, analytics, and 24/7 support. Other sites like Wix.com and Weebly.com offer some of the same DIY website-building services and ecommerce abilities.

On the flip side there are many business websites that could be far more effective if they were created by a professional. Today, your website may be one of the first impressions of your business. If you can develop a great first impression from a turnkey solution, go for it, but if your site is going to look amateurish, overloaded, or lack in user functionality, by all means don't skimp on paying a pro to get you up and running.

Once you know what tools and resources you'll use to create and manage the site, the next step is to organize your site's potential content into the various written components that will be pages of your site. Component number one will be your homepage, the very first page that visitors see when they type in your URL. This is where you present, in words and with photographs, what your business is all about and why they should look further into what you do. Look at other homepages and get a feel for which ones you like. Judge by content, photos, layout, and the overall look of the page. You will see some homepages that are overloaded or too crowded. Others are vague, like those TV commercials that you enjoy watching but have no idea what the product is. Remember, the homepage answers their question; "What can this business or person do for me?"

"A dream is just a dream. A goal is a dream with a plan and a deadline."
—Harvey Mackay, founder of Mackay Envelope Co.

Research Made Perfect

To create an effective website, you need to do your homework. Some good resources are:

- Entrepreneur.com offers Online Business How-to Guides (entrepreneur.com/topic/how-to-start-a-business/). This series of articles offers everything you need to know about starting, running, and growing your online business.
- Ecommerce Guide's: How to Start Your First Ecommerce Business (ecommerceguide.com/guides/starting-your-commerce-store/). These articles list everything you'll need to get your online store off the ground.

Next you'll want to focus on component number two, the "About Us" or "About Me" page. This is a concise recap of your business, including your mission statement, what you do, how you got to where you are, and whatever makes your business stand out from the crowd. You can then include product or services pages, testimonials, pricing, special offers, a blog, links to articles pertaining to what your business does, or even written articles about you or your business. There are many options. You can start with a few pages, then add as your business grows. Each component will be linked to an icon. Arrange all the icons depicting major content areas in the order you want them. Also make sure your contact information is on every page.

Offer your visitors content that's valuable, informative, and engaging—make it worth their while to spend time on your site. Provide regular opportunities for visitors to get more content. Whether you offer a blog, free electronic newsletter, a calendar of events, columns from experts, a contest, articles, or book reviews, your content and the site's structure become the backbone of your website.

As part of your website design, use graphics, colors, and fonts that make sense (not just to you but to your target audience and their mobile devices as well).

TIP

When creating and designing your web content, you won't go wrong if you follow three basic design rules:

1. Put the most important content near the top.
2. Eliminate extraneous words and visual clutter from the content.
3. Use headlines, icons, bullets, boldface words, and color only to draw attention to important content, not to distract or confuse the web surfer.

Subtle visual cues make all the difference in how visitors respond to your website. Surf around to research what combinations of fonts, colors, and graphics appeal to your audience, and incorporate pleasant and effective design elements into your site. Look at the sites of successful competitors for ideas. Originality can be great, but there's a reason customers keep flocking to the same sorts of color schemes and designs—they work.

To create a successful website, all the elements must work seamlessly. Having top-notch content is essential, but it must be displayed in a manner that's easy to understand, visually appealing, simple to navigate, and of interest to your target audience. How you present your information is important. It's not just about what you have to say, but also the manner in which you present that content that will either attract or repel your audience.

Finding the Host with the Most

Now that you have your site's design and content creation well underway, the next step is publishing your site on the web. For this, you have three basic options. The first is to host it yourself on a computer that can be dedicated as a web server (or a computer that's permanently connected to the internet) and has a dedicated broadband internet connection. This will prove costly to set up and maintain.

For most online businesses, this isn't the best option, at least in the beginning.

The second option is to use an established and reputable web hosting company, which stores and manages websites for businesses, among other services. There are several large and well-established web hosting companies that cater to a worldwide audience, including Bluehost, HostGator, Hostinger, Network Solutions, and GoDaddy.

Some companies, however, prefer local, small hosting providers because they offer a direct contact—especially important if your site goes down. Most of these companies also offer domain name services, which we mentioned above, so you can sign up when you choose your name.

Success by Design

For a successful website, follow these general dos and don'ts of site design.

Do:

- Make your site easy to navigate.
- Use a consistent look, layout, design, and feel throughout your site.
- Make sure your website works with all the popular web browsers (Edge, Safari, Firefox, Chrome, etc.)
- Test your website thoroughly on your computer and on other devices. Make sure all your links work and the fonts/colors and images are easily viewed on smaller screens. You'd be surprised by how pages may appear on different-sized screens. Also, if you have a shopping cart feature, make sure it works smoothly and quickly—speed counts when selling online. This includes adding your shipping charges immediately. When it comes to online checkout, Amazon has spoiled us.
- Avoid clutter; less is often more.

Don't:

- Use text and color combinations that are too busy or distracting. Anything that makes your site confusing or hard to read should be eliminated immediately.
- Allow the content or links on your website to become outdated; update, fine-tune, and proofread regularly.

A third option is to use a website turnkey solution. As we mentioned above, this is a company that provides all the site development tools and hosting services in one easy-to-use, low-cost, bundled service, which is entirely online-based. In other words, to create, publish, and manage your website, you don't need to install any specialized software, and no programming is required. Using an internet search engine, enter the phrase "website turnkey solution" or "ecommerce turnkey solution." Also, check out what's offered by Yahoo!, Google, GoDaddy, and eBay. On the positive side, these are less expensive options. On the negative side, this is the equivalent of buying "off the rack." You get what you need—functional but not unique. It all depends on your business needs.

Whether buying from a large or small provider, basic hosting service—along with standards like domain name registration and email accounts—starts at about $15 per month but can go up considerably, depending on your needs.

Still not sure which host to choose? Consider other variables like the amount of disk space allocated to you, available bandwidth, number of email services offered, customer service support availability, database support, and setup fees. For even more information, check out CNET editors' web hosting guide, with discount codes for some, at cnet.com/web-hosting.

How much space do you need on your hard drive to store your website? Generally, 2MB can hold several hundred text pages—fewer pages when images and multimedia content are included. Look for at least 500MB, which should be more than adequate for most situations, unless you will have a lot of photos or videos, which will require more. If you are unsure how much drive space or bandwidth you need, check with your website designer or computer consultant before you sign on a web server's dotted line. Also read a contract carefully to see whether your low initial rate will get higher every year. Be wary of offers that say "unlimited."

AHA!

If you know what you want to say but are not sure how to best say it, one option is to hire a copywriter to transform your idea into compelling text. You may also wish to experiment with generative (AI) writing tools that incorporate OpenAI like ChatGPT that can help create content for you. To begin to learn about the pros and cons of these tools consider checking out the article, "The Advantages and Disadvantages of ChatGPT" at https://www.entrepreneur.com/growth-strategies/the-advantages-and-disadvantages-of-chatgpt/450268

When seeking a host for your website, there are several questions you should ask:

1. *Is security included in the hosting plan?* Find out what kind of security they offer. Your web hosting service should have a Secure Socket Layer (SSL) certificate, which has become standard in the industry.
2. *Do they provide backups of your data and how often?*
3. *Is customer service available 24/7?* You also need to know the best way to reach them if the site goes down. Speaking of which, the site should have at least a 99.5 percent uptime rating.
4. *Do you own your website?* If they also offer web design, you should still own your site.
5. *Can they handle scalability?* If your site gets a significant increase in traffic or you add more photos or videos, can the site accommodate such growth?

Review what hosting services offer on their websites and make a list of questions to ask. Write down answers and compare. Remember, these services are designed to meet many different needs—make sure your specific requirements are met.

AHA!

Although most people are now comfortable with the web as a secure place for credit card transactions, a little reassurance doesn't hurt. Have whomever sets up your shopping cart component provide a message to customers that details your company's policy for protecting credit card information and customer/client privacy. And make sure you are keeping up with updates and changes in security. After all, you can leave a reassuring message; just make sure it is accurate.

Ka-ching

The best part of ecommerce is that customers do the work while you make the sales. You've probably noticed that companies of all sizes, from SOHOs to the Fortune 500, use sticks and carrots to encourage web usage vs. telephone support for all sorts of transactions. Every time you serve yourself on the internet, whether it's to purchase an airline ticket, a can of cat food, or 100 shares of stock, you've saved the seller money on salaries and, ultimately, office space and phone charges.

In fact, many ecommerce entrepreneurs turn to the web hosting companies we mentioned above to solve all their ecommerce needs, such as handling credit card transactions, sending automatic email messages to customers thanking them for their orders, and forwarding the order to them for shipping and handling—and, of course, domain registration and hosting.

Keeping Up Appearances

Unless you're careful when designing and programming your website, it might behave differently to different people. This is because web browsers, the software that enables net users to navigate the web, differ somewhat in how the websites they access perform. Make sure your website is fully compatible with Google Chrome (the most commonly used web browser) as well as Safari (from Apple), and Microsoft Edge among others.

Also make sure the content works well with the message you're trying to achieve (and that it is readable on every browser) and is either responsive (so the typography automatically adjusts on a range of devices) or at least looks good on smartphone and tablet screens, not just laptop and desktop computers.

So how do you know how your site is behaving? Whenever you have the chance to use computers with different browsers, check your site. Note differences in appearance, ease of navigation, and speed. Be sure to check compatibility with all browsers (and all versions of each browser) before launching your site. Nothing destroys your credibility like computer mishaps.

Meet the Expert: Eric Butow, Website Developer

Eric Butow is the owner of Butow Communications Group (BCG) in Jackson, California (butow.net). BCG offers website development, online marketing, and technical writing services. Eric has authored or co-authored 38 books, most recently *Ultimate Guide to Social Media Marketing* (Entrepreneur Press, 2020) and *Instagram for Business for Dummies, Second Edition* (Wiley, 2021).

Where do you even start when thinking about a website for your business?

As a website developer myself, I start with the WordPress platform as it's used by about 41 percent of all websites and growing. It's nice to use a content management platform that's flexible and has a lot of user support.

What is the most important factor to consider when deciding on a design?

The user experience. Storyboarding not only the design but how users will actually use your website, makes the site better for your users and helps your business make more money.

Are there any web design or web content writing fads/trends that people should avoid?

There are three. Writing too much copy on the site instead of "chunking" the information. Talking about what a company does instead of the customer's problem and how you solve it. Not incorporating websites into an overall marketing strategy that includes social media and branding.
What common web design pain points do you see most often?
Bad spelling, links that don't work, and not updating the website regularly.
What are some of your favorite business websites?
I have five sites and a bonus site: Unsplash, which is a good source for free stock photos; iStock and Shutterstock for a far wider variety of stock photos, illustrations, and videos; Typewolf for finding the right fonts and font combinations; WebDesign-Inspiration.com to see award-winning website designs to give you ideas for your site; HubSpot Grader to test the design of your site and get tips to improve it. The bonus: Digital Blasphemy, because we all need great computer-generated art for our desktops and social media profiles.

Another option is to incorporate an electronic shopping cart, which allows people to place their orders online and processes their credit card payment. A site using a shopping cart program should have these five components:

1. *Catalog.* Customers can view products, get information, and compare prices.
2. *Shopping cart.* The icon works like the real thing. It tracks all the items in the basket and can add or delete items as the customer goes along. It's like an online order form.
3. *Checkout counter.* The shopper reviews the items in their cart, makes changes, and decides on shipping preferences, gift-wrapping, and the like.
4. *Order processing.* The program processes the credit card (or payment option), verifies all information, and sends everything to the order and processing database for fulfillment.

5. *Real-time tax and shipping calculations.* Search for shipping calculator plug-ins that you can add to your shopping cart feature to make shipping calculations a breeze.

You can also incorporate a simple—and inexpensive—point-of-sale payment program like Square if you're using web hosts with which they are partners.

> **WARNING**
> You can create the most incredible website and incorporate cutting-edge content, but if your text is filled with grammatical errors, misspellings, inappropriate language, or misused words, it will immediately destroy your reputation and credibility. Make sure you edit and proofread your site before you launch it.

Final Check

You're almost ready to launch your online business (or the online component to your traditional business). Here's a checklist to keep you on track:

- [ ] Keep your online and ecommerce strategy in focus.
- [ ] Put full contact information on your homepage and at least some contact information on every page.
- [ ] Keep graphics clean and eye-catching.
- [ ] Make sure your website is free of glitches, typos, and dead ends that frustrate visitors. Check links often, and make sure every page on your site opens.
- [ ] Enable visitors to easily navigate the site.
- [ ] Make sure your website is in sync with the rest of your business.
- [ ] See how your website looks on various mobile devices and computer monitors.

Once your website is up and running, it's time to get to the really important jobs. The first is attracting visitors to your site (generating traffic) followed by encouraging them to become paying customers. Promoting and advertising your site properly, and on an ongoing basis, will be essential for its success.

AHA!

Here's another idea to give your customers peace of mind: Look into third-party certification seal programs, or accreditation programs, that let you post a symbol to signify that your website is using effective privacy practices. For example, the Better Business Bureau Online (bbb. org) can provide accreditation that means the BBB has determined that the business meets high standards, which includes a commitment to making a good faith effort to resolve any consumer complaints. You could also display the VeriSign seal, which verifies that your business has been approved to protect confidential information with industry-leading SSL encryption.

CHAPTER 3

Keep in Touch

Using Technology to Stay Connected

THESE ARE EXCITING TIMES for mobile entrepreneurs. Laptops are smaller and far more powerful, and sleek smartphones are capable of a wide range of wireless interactivity. In addition, the cost of traditional long-distance phone service has plummeted, and the option to use the internet as a phone (using voice over internet protocol, or VoIP) has become extremely viable for saving a fortune on calls (as well as making video conferencing an affordable option for everyone). Plus, you can make calls through multiple tablet and smartphone apps as well—for free.

Thanks to the wireless web, you can connect to the internet anywhere and anytime and have a high-speed connection from a laptop, netbook, smartphone, or tablet.

While the technology that allows us to communicate more effectively is becoming increasingly powerful, the price for all this power is decreasing. Today, just about any startup entrepreneur can afford the latest smartphone, laptop, or a new tablet with wireless connectivity. These technologies allow you to talk, video conference, email, send a Direct Message (DM) (which is essentially the term for an instant message), or even communicate in ways never before possible—from anywhere. You're no longer held down by cables or phone lines or the need to find wifi hotspots or electrical outlets. You can conduct business as efficiently as if you were sitting at your office desk.

TIP

When selecting a cell phone, smartphone, or tablet, don't just look at the equipment in terms of its features and functionality. Determine what types of service plans are available, what fees are associated with those plans, and what apps you might want to use. Most carriers offer unlimited plans that allow multiple devices for one price. You could have three or four smartphones or tablets connected to one unlimited plan for about $10 to $40 per additional line.

Do Your Homework

It's your responsibility to determine what it is that you need. Everyone's requirements are different. While a netbook might be the ultimate solution for one person, a full-powered laptop or the latest Apple iPad or Microsoft Surface tablet might be a more useful tool for someone else.

Once you pinpoint which technology is best for you, it's up to you to become proficient using it. For some, overcoming the learning curve associated with the latest technologies, as well as an inherent fear of them, is a debilitating hindrance. To ensure your success in today's business world, you must possess the knowledge, skills, and experience to fully use the latest emerging technologies and the well-established ones.

The best way to acquire this knowledge and proficiency is to read the equipment manuals, visit related websites that offer interactive tutorials, and invest some time in using your new equipment. For example, before loading your phone with crucial work-related data, spend some time using all its features without the fear of corrupting or losing important information.

As you invest the time and energy to learn about the latest tools, don't just buy the hottest gadget so your colleagues, clients, and customers will be impressed. Focus on which of these technologies will make you more organized, efficient, productive, and available to current and prospective customers. Determine which mobile technology will be the biggest time and money saver. To accomplish this goal, you'll need to study your current work habits and how you spend your time and then choose appropriate technologies so you can stay compatible and competitive in today's fast-paced work environment.

FYI

If you want to become proficient using an iPhone or iPad quickly, visit the Apple.com website and watch the video tutorials that explain how to use the most popular features. Samsung tablet users should check out Androidforums.com for tutorials and easy-to-understand how-to and getting-started information. With more businesses making cell phones and other mobile technology today, there has been an increased effort by these companies to provide guidance on how to use their products.

Just the Beginning

There are so many different technologies that can be used for communicating and staying connected, it's impossible to write about them all or to focus on the many ways they can be used in conjunction to make you work better and more efficiently.

For example, if you travel a lot for your business, you can have one single phone number that follows you anywhere in the world or that rings in certain places at certain times of the day or night. If you're not available to answer the phone, the caller will automatically be sent to voice mail, and that message can be listened to at your convenience or automatically translated into an email message and sent to your smartphone, laptop, iPad, or even your desktop computer. Many phone service companies—and now cable providers—offer "Follow Me" functionality, including Google Voice (google.com/voice).

Your cell phone, smartphone, notebook computer, netbook, or iPad can handle many tasks: It can be used as a plain old telephone or as a full-featured voice-mail system that also sends/ receives emails, and DMs, or in some cases, allows for real-time video conferencing . . . and that's just the beginning.

Talk Is Cheap

Technological advancements offer us cheap home and office phone systems, powerful mobile smartphones, mobile broadband (for high-speed internet access from virtually anywhere), plus various kinds of text messaging and video communications. In fact, research shows that more and more people are giving up their traditional landlines in favor of using wireless cell phone technology as their primary home or business phone line(s).

Whether you use a landline or cell phone, most service plans these days offer unlimited local and long-distance calling for a flat rate (typically $30 to $100 per month). Thus, from a business perspective, your telecom budget line item went from a variable to a fixed expense. Add in plummeting telecom costs, and you have what amounts to cold, hard cash in your pocket, plus much greater communication tools at your disposal.

Even the cost of internet access has dropped significantly in recent years, thanks to DSL, broadband, FIOS, and wireless 4G/5G technologies.

WARNING
Never send or read text messages, DMs, emails, or surf the web while driving—no matter how appealing the concept of multitasking in this situation might be. If you're distracted, even for a second, the conse-quences can be deadly. Put your phone down while you drive, any message can wait.

Which Smartphone Is the Smartest?

Smartphones (such as iPhones, Android, and Google phones) offer powerful and seamless voice and data communications capabilities—all from a single handheld device. You can use a smartphone for a wide range of tasks, including sending/receiving calls, voice mails, emails, texts, and DMs. You can also surf the web, and use it as a powerful GPS navigational system as well as a personal productivity tool for managing your contacts, schedule, expenses, and other data.

Choosing which smartphone is right for you is a matter of personal preference based on your unique work habits, communication and connectivity needs, and budget. Once you know how you'll be using your smartphone, consider what features and functionality you want and need and then take a look at the various iPhone, Android, Google, and other smartphone models available. (If you're going to have employees, consider compatibility issues as well to ensure data from your smartphone will be transferable to your staff and vice versa.)

Also, consider the phone's design, battery life, screen readability, keyboard size (or virtual keyboard), overall size and weight, and price. Also, ask about repair/replacement service plans, insurance options, and warranty. You might consider having a case for your phone since they are not infallible.

FYI

Don't have a cellular wireless card for your laptop computer and need wifi web access while on the go? Most hotels, airports, coffee shops, and bookstores offer free or fee-based wifi. You can quickly find local wifi hotspots throughout the United States or abroad on wififreespot.com or openwifispots.com.

While you should certainly consider the cost of the device when shopping for a smartphone, you'll also want to look at:

- What the various cell phone carriers (AT&T, T-Mobile, Verizon, etc.) offer in terms of monthly service plans
- The cost of the monthly service plan (with all the extras you'll want and need, such as unlimited talk minutes, data usage, and text messaging)
- The length of the service contract you'll need to commit to (usually two years); if you cancel prematurely, you'll be charged an early termination fee of $175 to $300 depending on the carrier
- The level of national and international roaming service offered, based on the areas where you'll use your smartphone the most

SAVE

To save money on cell phone usage and international roaming fees when traveling overseas, consider purchasing an inexpensive, prepaid cell phone or temporary SIM card in the country you're visiting. This means you pay for the phone or the SIM card and a predetermined number of talk minutes or data usage for a certain number of days or weeks.

Keep in mind that most U.S.-based cell phones and smartphones will automatically work when you travel overseas, thanks to international roaming. However, unless you have an international roaming plan, you'll be charged $2 to $5 (or more) per minute to make or receive calls while overseas, plus you'll be charged up to $1 for each text message sent/received and up to $20 (or more) per megabyte of data sent/received. If you plan to travel overseas and use your cell phone or smartphone, inquire about international roaming packages, which can save you a bundle if activated before you leave the country. Most cell providers offer international plans that lower costs and can save small businesses tens of thousands. Even large businesses can negotiate for better rates. Starting price (per month per line) has dropped into the $30 to $60 range.

Data Is King

The question is no longer what cell phone you have, but how much data are you packing? Carriers have all sorts of offers. For example, Verizon includes up to a 20GB hotspot (aka 20GB of data). To put that in context, 20GB of data would allow you, on average, to stream two hours of music, browse the web, or go on social media for two hours and stream an hour-long TV show every day for a month. Of course, you could simply use all the data on the internet for 240 hours per month. For many small-business owners, whose business is not primarily online, this can be sufficient.

You will also find many services that offer unlimited data plans, which sound like the panacea for those who regularly use a lot of data on their cell phones. Unfortunately, many of those boasting about unlimited data are often taken by surprise when that unlimited data comes with a speed limit. Suddenly your data may slow down considerably. Again, this will depend on your usage. If your business needs do not include streaming videos or a lot of Zoom calls with multiple people, you probably don't have to worry. Keep in mind that data may be king, but speed counts, too.

SAVE

Another option for international calling is to forgo a cell phone altogether and rely on a VoIP service, such as Zoom to make free (or really cheap) calls from your laptop computer or iPad, which is connected to a high-speed wifi internet connection in your hotel, for example. If you own an iPad or iPhone, you can also use wireless connections to Skype or video chat via programs like FaceTime, without incurring extra charges. Apps like Zoom and WhatsApp offer the same free or inexpensive teleconferencing and video services.

Wireless Wonders

All laptop computers and smaller netbooks allow users to connect to the web via wifi (assuming a wifi hotspot is available) or a wireless internet card.

A wireless internet card is a cell phone modem for your computer. It allows the computer to connect to the internet via a cell phone connection, so no wifi hotspot is required. You just need to be within the service area of a wireless data provider with whom you have a data plan.

All the wireless service providers offer wireless modem cards for laptop and netbook computers (if the computer doesn't have the technology built in).

These modems connect to the computer, usually via a USB connection. To gain wireless access to the web, you'll need to sign up for a provider's data-only service plan. This can cost $40 to $60 per month—less if you've got a wireless contract for your smartphone with the provider already—depending on the data amount you need.

You might be better off activating mobile wifi hotspot capabilities for your smartphone, which can cost as little as $20 (and most carriers now include hotspot capabilities with unlimited data plans). Keep in mind, with some carriers, when other devices are connected to your phone, you won't be able to make calls. Be sure to ask for details.

Adding a wireless modem and service plan to your laptop allows you to surf the web (via a high-speed 4G or 5G wireless connection) from anywhere there's wireless data service from your provider. You don't need to hunt down a wifi hotspot or connect your computer to a modem. This gives you tremendous freedom to access the web anywhere, anytime.

Lightweight Computing

While tablets aren't phones, they offer the ability to surf the web with a large screen from almost anywhere. The tablet is incredibly lightweight and portable. There's also a virtual keyboard, so you don't need a separate keyboard or mouse to use the unit, although you can buy a small external keyboard for about $30. Apps available for the iPad are office-friendly and becoming more so every day. Other manufacturers also offer apps for Windows, too.

DMing

Direct messaging (also referred to as DMing) allows people to communicate in real time without speaking. While cell phones allow us to roam freely and wirelessly, and offer real-time conversations, texting has pretty much surpassed talking on cell phones for many users.

DMing is used while you're online and surfing the web to instantly send text-based messages (and potentially attached files or links) to a recipient, who receives your DM instantly on their desktop computer, laptop, netbook, iPad, or smartphone (assuming it's connected to the web). To use DMs, both the sender and the receiver must participate in the same (or on a compatible) DM service, such as Hangouts from Google, WhatsApp, or Yahoo!. A real-time, text-based conversation can be held between two or more people.

The benefit to DMing is that you can participate in an unlimited number of conversations simultaneously; plus, it's quicker than picking up the phone or sending a full-length email. Text messaging works in much the same way as DMing; however, to send and receive a text message, you use a cell phone or smartphone. You can send a text message to anyone with a cell phone, as long as you know their phone number, regardless of what carrier they use, and assuming you both have a text messaging plan as part of your cell phone service.

Apple allows what they refer to as iMessages from Macs or iPads to work over wifi, which turns texting into messaging. You can text from a phone or computer. However, an iMessage text over wifi can only be between Apple-to-Apple devices. It won't work with non-Apple products so you will need to use standard text messaging.

Two popular apps provide such multifaceted communication tools, Slack and Discord. Slack, however, is billed as a workplace communication tool, while Discord is primarily used by gamers. In 2023 it has also seen increased adoption in other areas such as business teams, educational groups, and various online communities.

Slack, which has apps for mobile devices as well as laptops or desktops, allows you and your team to communicate remotely and work on projects together. It takes features from texting, emailing, and direct messaging and incorporates them into one communication tool. It also has individual channels, meaning you can be in a group chat while also taking or sending a private message on a separate channel—kind of like having two phone lines that can easily be used for text communications. Slack Calls (which include video calls) also let you talk with your team from your phone or computer, essentially acting as a conference call with texting capabilities all in one.

Small businesses can try out Slack for free. Plans with additional features run from roughly $80 annually per user on a Standard Plan (or $8 per user if you're paying for a single month) to $150 on an annual Plus Plan (or $15 for a single month).

Web Calling

Instead of using traditional phone lines to make and receive calls, anyone with any type of high-speed internet connection can take advantage of VoIP technology to make and receive calls from the web. Calls originating from the web can be placed without using phone lines, often at a fraction of the cost of making a traditional long-distance call (and sometimes free of charge, depending on the service you use).

Using a VoIP service gives you access to a wide range of calling services and features, from caller ID and voice mail to call forwarding and conference calling. As long as you have a stable, high-speed internet connection, the calls will be clear. There are many VoIP services that offer features of interest to entrepreneurs. For example, there's RingCentral (ringcentral.com), Skype (skype.com), magicJack (magicjack.com), and Vonage (vonage.com). You can find a worldwide list of VoIP providers by visiting voipproviderslist. com. For people who need to make international calls, either from the United States to an overseas country or who travel overseas and need to call home to the United States, VoIP offers a tremendous savings over traditional phone or cellular phone services. In fact, by using VoIP, you can typically call anywhere in the world, anytime, for less than a few cents per minute (and sometimes for free). With VoIP, you're assigned your own phone number, plus you can receive calls at that number any time you're connected to the internet—from anywhere—or have calls forwarded to your cell phone or a landline. Most VoIP services charge a flat monthly fee of up to $30 for unlimited service or waive the monthly fee but charge a low, per-minute fee per call.

Session Initiation Protocol (SIP) is a signaling protocol that enables VoIP by defining the messages sent between end points and managing the actual elements of a call, meaning it can discern when the message begins and ends and what type of message is being sent: voice, text, video, etc. SIP provides compatibility between VoIP apps and desk and conference phones. It can lower phone bills for businesses by as much as 60 percent. You'll also get improved sound quality (especially for multiple person calls), in addition to making call recording easy.

It's Your Turn

Technology is changing rapidly and almost daily. New devices and tools are constantly being introduced. New software upgrades to existing devices, such as the iPhone or Android, are allowing greater functionality.

If you want to be competitive in today's business world, it's no longer a matter of whether you need a smartphone and/or laptop (with wireless capabilities), or a tablet—it's a matter of which model you need right now and how you'll be able to get the most use out of each technology or device as you juggle your daily work and personal responsibilities, plus deal with the growing need to be accessible virtually 24/7.

This chapter offered just a short introduction to the communications and connectivity technology that's available. How you use this technology is up to you. So put on your thinking cap, be creative, and discover ways you can use it to become more productive, accessible, and competitive in today's business world.

New technologies and phone models are introduced almost every month. One of the best ways to learn about the latest gadgets, gizmos, and technologies businesspeople use to communicate is to do a Google search for whatever you need or, if you're interested in Apple products (e.g., the iPhone or iPad), visit an Apple Store. By visiting a retail store that showcases the latest products, you can try them firsthand, learn about their features, and easily compare pricing.

PART 2
Marketing

CHAPTER 4

Brand Building

How to Build Your Brand

YOU'RE REALLY EXCITED ABOUT YOUR NEW BUSINESS. But do you have a potential brand in the making?

Unfortunately, it's a question too many small-business owners ask far too late, or never ask at all—not a good idea in a world full of savvy consumers and big companies that have mastered the branding game. Great brands are all around us, and it's no accident they make us think of certain things. Think FedEx, and you think of overnight delivery. Apple brings to mind cutting-edge products, music, and must-have phones and devices.

Even celebrities are brands. Would you describe Bradley Cooper the same way you would describe Dwayne (The Rock) Johnson? Their differences—charming vs. gruff, refined vs. rough and rugged—help define their particular acting "brands" and let the public get a grasp on their personas. Corporate brands are no different. They have their own "personalities."

We like to categorize everything, whether we're talking about people, printers, or pizza places. Test this theory yourself. What draws you to one local business instead of another selling a similar product? One local restaurant might strike you as quaint and inviting; another might hit you as chaotic and overcrowded—even though both restaurants serve the same type of food. You're not alone if you find yourself categorizing each business you pass.

As a startup entrepreneur, you'll be branding whether you're trying or not. If you don't have a clear idea of what your new company is about, your potential customers will decide on their own—a risky move for a new company without many, or any, customers. You'll need to have a branding strategy in place before your launch or grand opening. However, before we start strategizing, let's answer the most basic question of all.

TIP

Make your company's website more than just a boring online brochure by adding an enewsletter, a weekly or biweekly blog, or a monthly podcast from the founder—anything that conveys your brand's personality and humanizes your company in the eyes of potential customers. People want to know whom they're buying from, especially if it's a new company. And if you're not offering this, remember your next competitor might be.

What Is Branding, Exactly?

Branding is a very misunderstood term. Many people think of branding as just advertising or a really cool-looking logo, but it's much more complex—and exciting, too.

- *Branding is your company's foundation.* It's not just about awareness, a trademark, or a logo. Branding is your company's reason for being, the synchronization of everything about your company that leads to consistency for you as the owner, your employees, and your potential customers. Branding meshes your marketing, public relations, business plan, packaging, pricing, customers, and employees.
- *Branding creates value.* If done right, branding makes the buyer trust and believe your product is somehow better than your competitors'. Generally, the more distinctive you can make your brand, the less likely the customer will choose another company's product or service even if yours is slightly more expensive. "Branding is the reason why

people perceive you as the only solution to their problem," says Rob Frankel, a branding expert and author of *The Revenge of Brand X: How to Build a Big Time Brand on the Web or Anywhere Else, Round 2* (Frankel & Anderson, 2010). "Once you clearly can articulate your brand, people have a way of evangelizing your brand."

- *Branding clarifies your message.* You have less money to spend on advertising and marketing as a startup entrepreneur, and good branding can help you direct your money more effectively. "The more distinct and clear your brand, the harder your advertising works," says Frankel. "Instead of having to run your ads eight or nine times, you only have to run them three times."

- *Branding is a promise.* At the end of the day, branding is the simple, steady promise you make to every customer who walks through your door or visits your website—today, tomorrow, and a year from now. Your company's ads and brochures might say you offer speedy, friendly service, but if customers find your service slow and surly, they'll walk out the door feeling betrayed. In their eyes, you promised something you didn't deliver, and no amount of advertising will ever make up for the gap between what your company says and what it does. Branding creates the consistency that allows you to deliver on your promise over and over again.

"Success is often achieved by those who don't know that failure is inevitable."
—Gabrielle "Coco" Chanel, founder of Chanel Inc.

Creating an Awesome Brand

When creating your brand, you will think about everything from your logo to color scheme to the tag line. You also need a memorable brand name, strong message, support system, and all the necessary legalities, like getting trademarked, in place.

But that's only the beginning of your branding process. To help you complete creating a spectacular brand, follow these four tips, says entrepreneur John Rampton, founder of financial information company Due.

1. *Consider how people see you.* Google yourself, your industry, and your line of business. Hold a focus group of close friends. Get a sense of the words associated with you and the line of business you're going into, and begin to get a picture of how you're seen—and want to be seen.

2. *Amplify yourself.* Use LinkedIn, Facebook, Twitter, Pinterest, and Instagram to amplify your message and further establish your brand. Real replies to your postings let you get a feel for how people are perceiving you on social media.

3. *Weave your brand into all you do.* Your brand should be apparent in how you blog online and interact with your community, and in your word choices when you speak to customers.

4. *Be consistent.* As a customer, think about the brands you are most loyal to. Chances are they've earned your trust because they are dependable. For example, Zappos is known for delivering superior customer service. Dropbox includes its signature hand-drawn blue-box logo on all its messaging. All your communications—online and off—should show your brand.

Building a Branding Strategy

Your business plan should include a branding strategy. This is your written plan for how you'll apply your brand strategically throughout the company over time.

At its core, a good branding strategy lists the one or two most important elements of your product or service, describes your company's ultimate purpose in the world, and defines your target customer. The result is a blueprint for what's most important to your company and to your customer.

Don't worry; creating a branding strategy isn't nearly as scary or as complicated as it sounds. Here's how:

- *Step one.* Set yourself apart. Why should people buy from you instead of the same kind of business across town or on the web? Think about the intangible qualities of your product or service, using adjectives like friendly, time-saving, fast, sincere, or flexible. Your goal is to own a position in the customer's mind so they think of you differently from the competition. "Powerful brands will own a word—like Volvo [owns] safety," says Laura Ries, an Atlanta marketing consultant and co-author of *The 22 Immutable Laws of Branding: How to Build a Product or Service into a World-Class Brand* (Harper Business, 2002). Which word will your company own? A new hair salon might focus on the adjective convenient and stay open a few hours later in the evening for customers who work late—something no other local salon might do. How will you be different from the competition? The answers are valuable assets that constitute the basis of your brand.

Advance Branding

You don't have to wait until you open your doors or launch your online business to start your branding campaign. In fact, you should start in advance so you can market your upcoming business. Post a concise version of your website, get your logo out and about, talk about your business on social media (don't promote, just work it into the conversation). Once you have discovered your brand, spread the news even before your business gets officially started.

- *Step two.* Know your target customer. Once you've defined your product or service, think about your target customer.

You've probably already gathered demographic information about the market you're entering, but think about the actual customers who will walk through your door or shop on your website. Who is this person, and what is the one thing they ultimately want from your product or service? After all, the customer is buying it because they have a need. What need can you fulfill for your customers?

- *Step three.* Develop a personality. How will you show customers every day what you're all about? A lot of small companies write mission statements that say the company will "value" customers and strive for "excellent customer service." Unfortunately, these words are all talk and no action. Dig deeper and think about how you'll fulfill your brand's promise, and provide value and service to the people you serve. If you promise quick service, for example, what will quick mean inside your company? And how will you make sure service stays speedy? If you use the words "discerning" or "luxurious," how will you provide such an atmosphere, and what will you do to offer a high-end product or personalized service? Along the way, you're laying the foundation of your hiring strategy and how future employees will be expected to interact with customers. You're also creating the template for your advertising and marketing strategy.

Your branding strategy doesn't need to be more than one page at most. It can even be as short as one paragraph. It all depends on your product or service and your industry. The important thing is that you answer these questions before you open your doors.

TIP

A lot of new companies try to be everything to everyone, but this strategy will make it impossible to communicate your brand. Instead, identify your most likely customer and build your brand on what this person wants.

In the Loop

Many companies, large and small, stumble when it comes to incorporating employees into their branding strategies. But to the customer making a purchase, your employee is the face of the company. Your employees can make or break your entire brand, so don't ever forget them. Here are a few tips:

- *Hire based on brand strategy.* Communicating your brand through your employees starts with making the right hires. Look to your brand strategy for help. If your focus is on customer service, employees should be friendly, unflappable, and motivated, right? Give new hires a copy of your brand strategy, and talk about it.
- *Set expectations.* How do you expect employees to treat customers? Make sure they understand what's required. Reward employees who do an exceptional job or go above and beyond the call of duty.
- *Communicate, then communicate some more.* Keeping employees clued in requires ongoing communication about the company's branding efforts through meetings, posters, training, and regular discussion. Never assume employees can read your mind.

Bringing It All Together

Congratulations—you've written your branding strategy. Now you'll have to manage your fledgling brand. This is when the fun really begins. Remember, FedEx was once a startup with an idea it had to get off the ground, too. Here are some tips:

- *Keep ads brand-focused.* Keep your promotional blitzes narrowly focused on your chief promise to potential customers. For example, a new bakery might see the warmth of its fresh bread as its greatest brand-building asset. Keep your message simple and consistent so people get the same message every time they see your name and logo.

- *Be ruthlessly consistent in all you do.* Filter every business proposition through a branding filter. How does this opportunity help build the company's brand? How does this opportunity fit our branding strategy? These questions will keep you focused and put you in front of people who fit your product or service.
- *Shed the deadweight.* Good businesses are willing to change their brands but are careful not to lose sight of their original customer base and branding message. Consider Starbucks, which changed the way it made lattes to speed up the process. "You have to give up something to build a brand," Ries says. "Good brands constantly get rid of things that don't work."

There's a lot of work that goes into launching and building a world-class brand, but it pays off. Nike once ran its business out of the back of a car, but now it's a global brand worth billions of dollars. Think of your fledgling brand as a baby you have to nurture, guide, and shape every day so it grows up to be dependable, hardworking, and respectable in your customers' eyes. One day, your company's brand will make you proud. But you'll have to invest the time, energy, and thought it takes to make that happen.

Many Happy Returns?

It can be hard to put a dollar figure on what you're getting in return for your investment in branding. Branders talk about this dilemma in terms of *brand equity*: The dollar value your brand generates over decades in terms of the demand it drives and the customer loyalty it creates. Coca-Cola's brand equity, for example, is estimated in the billions of dollars.

Think about conducting a simple brand audit at least once a year. This means looking at how your product or service is marketed and branded (your marketing messages, etc.), analyzing your brand positioning (i.e., asking customers what they think of your brand), and then comparing the two (your branding efforts vs. customer perceptions) to see how well the two connect.

A simple customer survey with questions like "When you think about our company and our product, what words come to mind?" can tell you volumes about the strengths and weaknesses of your branding.

A new coffee shop owner, for example, might think they serve the best coffee in town, but convenience and ambience are also part of the customer's experience. The convenience of the location, the type of music played over the sound system, and/or the comfortable seating that's conducive for working might be as much, or more, of a selling point from the customer's perspective. A brand audit will help keep you on track and build on what you already do well. Plus, it can help you tweak where you put your money and efforts, not just for branding, but also marketing and your actual product or service.

Being good at branding means being flexible, not stubborn. If people are looking for a healthier menu, for instance, give them one. Today, fast-food restaurants are extending their brand to include healthy menu options, while not departing from fast service and affordable prices. McDonald's, for example, has stuck to their brand, but they have added apple slices to their kids' meals. Flexibility means maintaining your brand while adjusting it to the changing world.

Read All About It

Luckily, there are tons of books on the topic of branding. Here are just a few of them, along with a major trade magazine:

- *Sticky Branding: 12.5 Principles to Stand Out, Attract Customers and Grow an Incredible Brand* (Dundurn, 2015). Written by Jeremy Miller, this book focuses on simplicity, taking it slow, and being bold when necessary.

- *Designing Brand Identity: A Complete Guide to Creating, Building, and Maintaining Strong Brands* (Wiley, 2006). This book by Alina Wheeler discusses branding fundamentals and also provides a number of case studies.
- *Emotional Branding: The New Paradigm for Connecting Brands to People* (Allworth Press, 2010). Written by Marc Gobé, this book delves into creating a strong brand personality, among other things.
- *Brand Identity Breakthrough: How to Craft Your Company's Unique Story to Make Your Products Irresistible* (Identity Publications, 2016). Author Gregory V. Diehl provides a host of information, from telling your own story and creating your brand identity to getting your message out there.
- *How to Launch a Brand (2nd Edition): Your Step-by-Step Guide to Crafting a Brand: From Positioning to Naming and Brand Identity* (Brandtro, 2016). Fabian Geyrhalter authors this straightforward approach to brand building, using his two decades of taking product and service ideas and turning them into brands.

CHAPTER 5

Genius Marketing

Advertising and Marketing
Your Business

You may know how to build, and/or buy and sell, the perfect products or provide excellent services, but do you know how to market your business? If not, all your expertise won't keep your business afloat. Without marketing, no one will know your business exists—and if customers don't know you're there, you won't make any sales.

Advertising doesn't have to mean multimillion-dollar TV commercials. There are plenty of ways to market your business that are affordable and even free. All it takes is a little marketing savvy and the dedication to stick with a year-round program that includes a solid mix of proven tactics.

"If you can dream it, you can do it."
—Walter Elias Disney, founder of Walt Disney Co.

Creating a Marketing Plan

Unlike a business plan, a marketing plan focuses on winning and keeping customers. A marketing plan is strategic and includes numbers, facts, and objectives. Marketing supports sales, and a good marketing plan spells out all the tools and tactics you'll use to achieve your sales goals. It's your plan of action—what you'll sell, who will want to buy it, and the tactics you'll use to generate leads that result in sales. And unless you're using your marketing plan to help gain funding, it doesn't have to be lengthy or beautifully written; it's better to use bulleted sections and get to the point.

Step One: Begin with a Snapshot of Your Company's Current Situation, Called a "Situation Analysis"

This first section of the marketing plan defines your company and its products or services and then shows how the benefits you provide set you apart from your competition.

Target audiences have become extremely specialized and segmented. For example, there are hundreds of special-interest websites and magazines—each targeted to a specific market segment. No matter your industry, from restaurants to retail clothing stores to providing professional services, positioning your product or service competitively requires an understanding of your niche market. Not only do you need to be able to describe what you market, but you must also have a clear understanding of what your competitors are offering and be able to show how your product or service provides a better value.

Make your Situation Analysis a succinct overview of your company. You can do this using a basic SWOT analysis, which stands for Strengths, Weaknesses, Opportunities, and Threats. Strengths and weaknesses refer to characteristics that exist within your business, while opportunities and threats refer to outside factors. To determine your company's strengths, consider the ways that your products or services are superior to others, or if your service is more comprehensive, for example. What do you offer that gives your business a competitive advantage? Weaknesses, on the other hand, can be anything from operating in a highly saturated market to lack of experienced staff members. To do this effectively you should perform a competitor analysis whereby you identify your most direct competitors, which can include both brick-and-mortar operations and online businesses. Research their products, prices, services, and sales and marketing strategies. By studying what they are doing well and looking for places where you can provide better products, prices, services, value, or all of the above, you can greatly improve your position in the market. Remember, you want to set yourself apart from the competition, so take your time to determine what they do well and what they are missing.

Next, describe any external opportunities you can capitalize on, such as an expanding market for your product. Don't forget to include any external threats to your company's ability to gain market share so that succeeding sections of your plan can detail the ways you'll overcome those threats.

Positioning your product involves two steps. First, you need to analyze your product's features and decide how they distinguish your product from its competitors. Second, decide what type of buyer is most likely to purchase your product. What are you selling—convenience? Quality? Discount pricing? You can't offer it all. Knowing what your customers want helps you decide what to offer, and that brings us to the next section of your plan. Be clear about this so you can keep coming back to it when you're tempted to try to do more than you should.

Position Power

The right image packs a powerful marketing punch. To make it work for you, follow these steps:

- Create a positioning statement for your company. In one or two sentences, describe what distinguishes you from your competition.
- Test your positioning statement. Does it appeal to your target audience? Refine it until it speaks directly to their wants and needs.
- Use the positioning statement in every written communication to customers.

- Integrate your company's positioning message into all your marketing campaigns and materials.
- Include your team in the positioning effort. Help employees understand how to communicate your positioning to customers.

TIP

Your business plan and your marketing plan have a lot in common, but make sure to keep them separate. Your business plan should show how you're going to support your marketing efforts. At the same time, your marketing plan should be a concrete working-out of the ideas in your business plan.

Step Two: Describe Your Target Audience

Developing a simple, one-paragraph profile of your prospective customer is the second step in creating an effective marketing plan. You can describe prospects in terms of demographics—age, sex, family composition, earnings, and geographic location—as well as lifestyle. Ask yourself the following: Are my customers conservative or innovative? Leaders or followers? Timid or aggressive? Traditional or modern? Introverted or extroverted? How often do they purchase what I offer? In what quantity? What makes them buy? How do they make most purchases (online/in person)? And perhaps most significantly, what are their wants and needs? After all, this is where you come into the picture as a business with products and/or services that can meet those wants and needs.

If you're a business-to-business marketer, you may define your target audience based on their type of business, job title, size of business, geographic location, or any other characteristics that make them possible prospects. Are you targeting the owners of businesses with 25 or fewer employees or midlevel managers in Fortune 100 companies? No matter who your target audience is, be sure to narrowly define them in this section because it will be your guide as you plan your media and public relations campaigns. The more narrowly you define your target audience, the less money you'll waste on ads and PR in poorly targeted media and the unqualified leads they would generate.

Research today is done primarily online, although you shouldn't hesitate to make a few phone calls if you think you can get more precise answers. Among the best sources of information will be the U.S. Census tools (census.gov/data/data-tools.html), the Pew Research Center (pewresearch.org), Statista (statista.com), Alexa Tools (alexa.com), Google Surveys (surveys.google.com), SurveyMonkey (surveymonkey.com), or by Googling the SBA's office of Entrepreneurship Education.

WARNING

Don't mess with success. Once you find an advertising idea that works for you, stick with it. Repetition is the key to getting your message across. Conversely, if something isn't working, put a stop to it quickly—don't take a wait-and-see approach. You want your money and effort going toward what works.

Step Three: List Your Marketing Goals

What do you want your marketing plan to achieve? For example, are you hoping for a 20 percent increase in sales of your product per quarter? Write down a short list of goals—and make them measurable so that you'll know when you've achieved them. Think SMART Goals, which stands for Specific, Measurable, Attainable, Relevant, and Time-bound, as in setting a time frame by which you will complete your goals.

Step Four: Develop the Marketing Communications Strategies and Tactics You'll Use

This section is the heart and soul of your marketing plan. In the previous sections, you outlined what your marketing must accomplish and identified your best prospects; now it's time to detail the tactics you'll use to reach these prospects and accomplish your goals.

A good marketing program targets prospects at all stages of your sales cycle. Some marketing tactics, such as advertising, public relations, and blog postings are great for reaching cold prospects. Warm prospects—those who have previously been exposed to your marketing message and perhaps even met you personally—will respond best to permission-based email, social media posts, loyalty programs, and customer appreciation events, among others. Your hottest prospects are individuals who've been exposed to your sales and marketing messages and are ready to close a sale. Generally, interpersonal sales contact (whether in person, email, or text) combined with marketing adds the final heat necessary to close sales.

To complete your tactics section, outline your primary marketing strategies and then include a variety of tactics you'll use to reach prospects at any point in your sales cycle. For example, you might combine online and print advertising and online local searches to reach cold prospects, but use email to contact your warm prospects. Finally, you can set up one-on-one conversations on video communications platforms like Zoom (zoom.com), or in-person meetings to close the sale. Don't overlook complementary materials that support sales: For instance, if you plan to meet with prospects to follow up on leads you've generated, you'll need brochures and presentation materials. Of course, all this has to conform to your products, services, and pricing. If you are selling smaller items, you'll want to get the attention of a mass (targeted) audience. In other words, you don't see McDonald's representatives sitting down with individual clients, but you will see a sales rep from a car or boat dealership ready to sit down with a potential customer once they've got one in the showroom.

To identify your ideal marketing mix, find out which media your target audience turns to for information on the type of product or service you sell. Avoid broad-based media—even if it attracts your target audience—if the content is not relevant. The marketing tactics you choose must reach your prospects when they'll be most receptive to your message.

Step Five: Set Your Marketing Budget

You'll need to devote a percentage of projected gross sales to your annual marketing budget. Of course, when starting a business, this may mean using newly acquired funding, borrowing, or self-financing. Just bear this in mind—marketing is essential to the success of your business. And with so many kinds of tactics available for reaching out to every conceivable audience niche, there's a mix to fit even the tightest budget.

As you begin gathering costs for the marketing tactics you outlined in the previous section, you may find that you've exceeded your budget. Not to worry. Simply go back and adjust your tactics until you have a mix that's affordable. The key is to never stop marketing. Don't concern yourself with the more costly tactics until you can afford them. Smart, targeted marketing doesn't have to cost a fortune.

So what should you spend on marketing? There's no hard-and-fast guideline. In fact, the amount varies based on your industry, the amount of competition you must overcome, and the type of media you have to use to reach your audience. A particularly complex message will also require a bigger marketing budget because prospects will need to be guided through the education phase, which involves more advertising and an increase in the repetition of your message. One study showed that major advertisers with well-established brand names, including General Mills, Dunkin', and Kraft Heinz, spend an average of 12 percent of sales on marketing. On the other hand, many successful small businesses that are competing for brand recognition and market share budget approximately 15 to 20 percent of sales. The rule of thumb: The SBA recommends spending 7 to 8 percent of your gross revenue for marketing and advertising if you're doing less than $5 million a year in sales and your net profit margin—after all expenses—is in the 10 percent to 12 percent range.

TIP

Dream the dream. Your marketing plan should include a "blue sky" section in which you put your feet up and look at where you think you'll be in a couple of years. Especially in small businesses, it's a waste of time to formulate marketing thoughts that go out more than two or three years. But dreams are important—and they can be fun and inspiring as well.

Start Early—Earlier Than You Think

Your marketing efforts should begin even before a product or service launch. After you figure out when you plan to launch, work backward to create a schedule that is as specific and detailed as possible, and use it to initiate a smart, quick prelaunch marketing campaign.

Use this period to build anticipation among your audience for your service or product. You can track social media interactions with your campaign using social media tracking sites such as Buffer (buffer.com) or Hootsuite (hootsuite.com). If you find that the target audience is skeptical or concerned about specific product details, take that feedback and apply it preemptively, and you'll ensure that customer expectations are met and avoid negative feedback at launch.

Here are four strategies you can implement when cultivating the early marketing plans for your business:

1. *Make sure your product stands out.* Let the target market know how the product is different from the competition by using data to locate the right audience and communicate with them consistently.
2. *Speak the language of your audience.* Don't launch your product with a blanket campaign that tries to reach everyone. Understand your key demographics—everything from age to attitude to geolocation to shopper type—and coordinate your marketing plan by triangulating that information with similar data on various marketing platforms.
3. *Evolve your strategy as necessary.* As you deploy and test your initial marketing goals, take heed of what the audience is responding to. This will help you figure out how and where your efforts should be targeted. Don't be afraid to tweak and evolve your campaign as you receive this feedback.
4. *Don't be afraid to kill your darlings.* Even with astute strategizing, not all marketing plans are successful. If the promotions from a campaign launch aren't going to pan out, re-evaluate and reposition your marketing plan before you've spent too much money on something unsuccessful, even if it was an idea you loved. And if a particular campaign fails to get results, adjust the format and rewrite the copy. If the situation still doesn't improve, move on to a new sales approach, possibly a new iteration of the product, or even a different product or business altogether.

Where to Advertise

Once you know your target audience, it will be easier to determine which media will work well for you. Much of this is common sense based on your product or service, method of sales, and audience.

Sure, it would be great if you could afford to buy a full-page color ad in *Time* magazine or a 60-second commercial during the Super Bowl. But in addition to being beyond your budget, such ads aren't the most effective way to go for a small company to succeed.

Small companies succeed by finding a niche, not by targeting every Tom, Dick, and Harry. Similarly, you need to focus your advertising as narrowly as possible on the media that will reach your customers. Your customers' location, age, income, interests, and other information will guide you to the right media.

Suppose you ran a business selling model train supplies nationwide online. It would make sense to advertise in a mix of national specialty magazines, on websites targeting aficionados, and in specialty newsletters catering to the hobby rather than advertising in, say, *The New York Times*. On the other hand, if you sold model trains from a hobby shop rather than online or via mail order, most of your customers would be drawn from your local area. Therefore, advertising in national hobbyist magazines would net you only a few customers. In this case, it would make more sense to advertise on local websites, area newspapers or in magazines that carry related editorial sections online and/or in print, with fliers distributed around the area, or by commercials on carefully selected cable TV programming targeting the local area. And don't forget signage. From a bench to a bus to a billboard, local businesses can benefit from traffic (on foot or by car) seeing the name of your business. Also, don't forget social media. It's likely that your customers are on social media platforms, so give them the chance to find you there. (See below).

Like any aspect of running a business, marketing involves a measure of trial and error. As your business grows, however, you'll quickly learn which advertising media are most cost-effective and draw the most customers to your company. Here's a closer look at the different types of advertising methods and tips for succeeding with each.

"All you need in this life are ignorance and confidence, and then success is sure."
—Mark Twain

Digital Advertising

Inevitably digital advertising has grabbed the crown away from traditional advertising as the most used form of spreading the word about businesses. Digital advertising uses online platforms, such as social media, search engines, and websites to reach a target audience, and it does so quickly and with the flexibility to alter messages for different audiences. Not only can you reach people on the internet, where most people are searching for information, products, services, solutions, and a way to meet their needs, but you can also manage, track, analyze, and improve advertising campaigns quickly and seamlessly. And with the right tools, well-placed ads can lead directly to sales without your target audience having to leave the comfort of their own homes.

There are several ways to run digital advertising campaigns, one of which is the popular pay-per-click (PPC) method by which you pay a small fee for every click on your ad, which should link directly to your website. Paid search is the most common method of PPC advertising. When people search Google or another browser, and click on your ad, you will be charged an agreed-upon cost (in your contract). This rate will vary depending on several factors as determined by the search engine. There are also PPC display advertisements and other PPC options. While PPC advertising can be a wonderful way of drawing customers, you must stay within a budget that works for you, no matter what people at a social media platform suggest you use as a budget. Remember, they are trying to make money through sales, so they will want you to boost your ads beyond your more realistic budget. It is, therefore, best to start slowly with a limited budget—carefully learn how to select the market you want to reach out to, test a few ads with different keywords, and alter your tactics as you monitor the results. Like most types of advertising, PPC takes time to work, so be cautious with your budget and make it last, because effective advertising takes time.

You can also use social media ad postings, such as placing ads on Facebook, LinkedIn, or other popular platforms. These sites offer numerous advertising options. Over the years, online advertising tools have made it easier to home in on your target market. Therefore, you don't have to advertise to millions of Facebook members—only to those who fit your specific demographic.

Want to Have a Mouthpiece?

Try an influencer. For years, companies have been hiring celebrities to help them market their products. You can do the same thing. A variety of online influencers can be found across social media platforms, and for a price, they can post comments, write blog posts, talk about, or include your business in any number of ways. The larger the influencer's reach and the more followers they have, the more possible prospects they can attract to your business. Of course, the better known they are, the more they will charge.

Brand influencers have built a rapport with their audience, and if their audience matches yours, they may be the influencer to speak up on behalf of your business. You don't necessarily need a major celebrity to help you hawk your goods or services—simply someone who's trusted and known to your niche audience. It's surprising how many people will follow the lead and advice of their online heroes—but they do. Hint: Let a brand influencer do their thing. If you try to script them too much, they will lose that special appeal that makes their audiences love and trust them.

Influencer marketing has evolved in recent years into a multi-billion-dollar industry. For your small niche business, you don't need an influencer with a million followers. You may do fine with someone who has 25,000 followers with a perfect market for what you sell. These are called micro-influencers—they charge less and are not A-list celebrities, but they reach out to the people with whom you want to connect. You can find influencers who are well-known, respected, and trusted in any type of business. There are various other types of influencers, with the top tier being the macro-influencers. These are notable names on social media platforms with at least 250,000 followers. While such numbers are impressive, they cannot reach out as personally as the micro-influencers. Nonetheless, if you want to, and can afford to, reach a larger group with a more "mainstream" product or service, macro-influencers can be helpful.

While many business owners have seen a spike in sales thanks to influencers, it's harder to track the results and ROI of an influencer as opposed to getting the data on PPC or other forms of digital marketing. If your influencer has included you in their blog, or you've made a video together, you can see how many people have seen the video or read the blog. If they have posted on your behalf, you can also see the number of people who have engaged with them.

Because digital marketing is the king of advertising and marketing in the third decade of the new century, it's important to start out with an awareness of the many opportunities.

Digital Advertising Advantages

It's always been difficult to determine how many people are seeing your ad in a newspaper, magazine, or on a sign or billboard. Digital advertising on major search engines and social media platforms gives you a means of tracking how many people saw your ads and clicked through to your website. You can then drill down and get a host of statistics on how long they stayed on your site, which pages they visited, etc. As a result, you can analyze and retool your advertising as never before.

Print Advertising

Knowing the principles of creating print ads will help you get results in any other advertising media you use. After all, the message is the same across different mediums. Print ads have helped launch some of the most successful products and services we know. And there's no reason they can't work for you, too—if you observe a few hard-and-fast rules.

There are certainly some cries that print advertising is dead or ineffective. But recently neuroscientists have reported that print ads make a better impression than digital.

Most print ads out there are poorly conceived and, as a result, perform badly. If an ad lacks a strong motivating message, it becomes a costly lesson—one your business will be lucky to survive. The good news? With so many bad ads out there, if you can put together a good one, you're way ahead of the game.

TIP

Make sure all your ads answer every customer's number-one question: What's in it for me?

Whether you are developing an ad yourself or having someone else craft it for you, make sure it follows the five fundamentals of successful ads.

1. *It should attract attention.* That sounds obvious, but nothing else matters unless you can do this. And that means having a truly arresting headline and an accompanying visual element.

2. *It should appeal to the reader's self-interest or announce news pertinent to them.* An ad that takes the "you" point of view and tells readers how they'll benefit from your product or service piques and keeps their interest. And if, in addition, it has news value ("Announcing a bold new breakthrough in moisturizers that can make your skin look years younger"), your ad has a better than fighting chance.

3. *It should communicate your company's unique advantage.* In other

words, why should the prospect pick your firm over a competitor's?

4. *It should prove your advantage.* Two convincing ways to do that are through testimonials and statistics.
5. *It should motivate readers to act.* This is usually accomplished by making a special offer that "piggybacks" your main sales thrust. Such offers include a free trial, a discount, or a bonus.

An ad doesn't have to do a "hard sell" as long as it is an all-out attempt to attract, communicate with, and motivate the reader. That process starts with the single most important element of any ad: the headline.

Headlines That Work

Some of the biggest flops in advertising contained convincing copy that never got read because the ads lacked a great headline or visual element to hook the passing reader.

Legendary David Ogilvy, founding partner of legendary ad agency Ogilvy & Mather, said that on the average, five times as many people read the headlines of ads as read the body copy (more recently, this has proved true for email newsletters and marketing blasts as well). Headlines that work best, according to Ogilvy, are those that promise the reader a benefit—today that translates as time-saving, faster results, more accurate, healthier, etc.

Increasingly, that means personalizing them in some way, to make the reader feel you understand them and the problem or issue your product or service helps them solve.

Go for the Pros

Can you create your own advertising copywriting and design? If you have a background in marketing and advertising, the answer may be yes. If not, however, you're better off hiring professionals.

No matter how creative you are, a commercial artist or a graphic designer can vastly improve almost any ad created by an entrepreneur.

However, because no one knows your business better than you, it's a good idea to develop your own rough draft first. Think about the key benefits you want to get across, what makes your company different from and better than the rest, and the major advantages of doing business with you.

If you're reluctant to spend the money on a copywriter and a graphic designer, don't be. Printing, distributing, and placing your advertising and marketing materials is going to be costly. If the materials you're paying to distribute (in print or online) aren't well-written, eye-catching, and effective, you're wasting your time and money.

Graphic design and copywriting are two areas where it's possible to get good work at substantial savings. Plenty of freelance, one-person graphic design and copywriting businesses exist, many of them quite reasonably priced. Ask friends, other business owners, or your chamber of commerce for referrals. Many copywriters and designers will cut you a price break on the first project in hopes of winning your business in the future. Of course, the old saying "you get what you pay for" should always be in the back of your mind. Paying $5 for someone to design your ad may be cheap, but it's also a waste of time. Your ads are important; pay for good people to help you with your design and content—it's well worth it.

What's more, in an attempt to keep companies from going all-digital on ads, some publishers have staffed-up their own ad departments with graphic and design teams who can help clients create smarter advertisements as part of the cost of buying an ad.

Flip through a magazine or look at ads online and see what stands out about them. Typically, your eyes go to the headline first. Then notice how many of those headlines promise a benefit.

However, expressing a benefit is not enough if the way you communicate it is dull and hackneyed. Your headline should be unusual or arresting enough to get interest. Here are some examples of headlines that got noticed:

- "When doctors feel rotten, this is what they do."
- "Why some foods explode in your stomach."
- "How a fool stunt made me a star salesman."
- "The one thing you need to do today to make your money last."

John Caples, co-author of the classic guide *Tested Advertising Methods, Fifth Edition* (Prentice Hall, 1998), recommends beginning headlines with such words or phrases as "New," "Now," "At last," "Warning," or "Advice" to pique interest. Timeliness and personalization ("Today" and "Your") are also effective in today's fast-paced world. Nobody wants to miss out. Numbers are also eye catchers . . . just look at the numbers on magazine covers by the checkout at the grocery store.

Whatever you do, don't use your company name as the headline. This is one of the most common mistakes small companies make. Would you read an ad with the headline "Brockman Financial Services"? Probably not. You can, however, tie your company name to an achievement, such as "Nina's Nails Offers First Drive-Thru Manicures."

TIP

Can't come up with ideas for your ad? Try a brainstorming session. Jot down words or phrases related to your product or service and its benefits. Then see what associations they trigger. Write down all the ideas you can think of without censoring anything. From those associations—whether words, phrases, or visual images—come ideas that make good ads.

Ads That Stand Out

Imagine scanning a convention half full of people dressed in formal attire and suddenly noticing that one brazen attendee is wearing overalls and a red flannel shirt. Is it safe to say your eyes would be riveted to that individual? Your first reaction might be "How dare he?" But you'd also probably be curious enough to walk over and find out what this audacious character was all about.

Such nonconformity can have the same riveting effect in advertising. Imagine scanning a newspaper page full of ho-hum little ads, then noticing that one of them stands out from the crowd. Suddenly, the other little ads become invisible and the unique one grabs all the attention. That ad has accomplished the single most difficult task small-business advertising faces—simply getting noticed.

Ideally, your advertising should reflect your company in both look and message. An ad represents you and what you have to offer. If it's generic, it won't have the power to grab attention or persuade prospects to take action.

Even a small ad, if it exhibits something a little unexpected, can steal the thunder of larger, more traditional ads. But what can you say in a small space that gets noticed and makes an impression? Here are a few ideas that could work with a variety of products or services:

- *For a restaurant*: Use a large but short headline that can't help but arouse curiosity, such as "Now, that's enormous!" This would then be followed by an explanation that this is usually the reaction when one of Francisco's Super-Subs (or whatever large-serving entrée) is placed in front of a customer.
- *For a car dealership*: Cars usually sell themselves, so you'll need to think outside the box to get people's attention. One luxury car company posted a headline above a photo of a car that read: "Protected by more prenups than any other car."

- *For a jewelry store*: In a jewelry store, it is often the case that the buyer is looking for a gift rather than being the one to wear it. One jewelry store used this approach with a photograph of an expensive ring and an ad geared toward male buyers that read: "Make her forget every anniversary you've ever forgotten."

Ad Placement

The print world has long consisted of two major entities: newspapers and magazines. For decades many people read the daily papers and even more read the Sunday papers. In recent years, the newspaper industry has seen a rapid decline. In fact, in 2018 newspaper circulation fell to its lowest numbers in nearly 80 years since 1940, when such circulation data first became available. Unfortunately, the numbers have continued to decline, with readers turning to the digital editions of the major players.

For a small business, local papers can still be worthwhile, especially those papers that maintain a decent following for their online editions. Ad placement can be particularly effective in the digital versions of local papers. The positive aspects of local digital and/or print newspapers are that you can reach a diverse audience and typically get good rates because most papers are struggling for readership. The digital versions also allow you to make changes and updates quickly and easily and include better visuals than you ever could in print versions. Your ads can appear rather quickly, which enables you to run an ad, for example, that capitalizes on some market turn of events that saves your prospects money if they act fast and buy from you now. The larger papers have a loyal, trusted following, but they will cost you more money.

The Good Word

Third-party praise—whether from a customer, an industry organiza-tion, or a publication—is one of the most effective tools you can use to give your advertising added credibility. This can take a variety of forms:

- If your business has received some kind of prize, mention in the press, or other honor, don't hesitate to put it in your advertising. "Rated #1 by Dog Groomers Monthly" or "Voted 'Best Value' by The Chagrin Falls Gazette" are good ways to establish your product or service's benefit in customers' eyes.
- Testimonials from individual customers carry weight, too. "Wanda's Party Planners Gave My Son the Best Birthday Ever! — *Jane Smith, Wichita, Kansas*," attracts customers' attention. How to get testimonials? If a customer says something nice about your business, don't let the compliment slide—ask, then and there, if you can use the testimonial in your sales materials. (You'll want to get this in writing just to be on the safe side.) Most customers will be happy to comply. Hint: Do not make up fake testimonials—you totally risk your credibility!
- Even if your company hasn't gotten recognition, perhaps you can use a part, a process, or an ingredient from one of your suppliers that has received praise. For example, you could say "Made with the Flame Retardant Rated #1 by the American Fire Safety Coun-cil." This tells your customers you think highly enough of them to provide them with such a great product or ingredient.
- If you're a member of the Better Business Bureau, that's an implied endorsement, too. Be sure to post your BBB plaque prominently on your store or office wall or use the logo on your letterhead. If the BBB has given you a good grade (B+ or better), you can also post your grade in your advertising.

As for placement, newspapers are typically categorized, so you can look for the subject area that your audience is most likely to read.

For example, if you own a sporting goods store you might want your ad on the sports pages, or if your business deals with fashion, look to place your ad on the fashion or style pages. While design options have been limited in newspapers, you do have the opportunity to get your name in front of prospective local customers.

Just as with most media, your budget must allow for running your ad with enough frequency for its message to penetrate. Regular exposure of the ad builds recognition and credibility. If some of your prospects see your ad but don't respond to your first insertion, they may well respond to your second or third. If you have confidence in your ad's message, don't panic if the initial response is less than what you wanted. Repetition is a key to successful advertising. Repetition is a key to successful advertising. Point made.

The second type of publication is magazines, and unlike the steady demise of the printed newspaper, magazines have held up well despite the internet. While statistics show that people will spend much less time reading or browsing through a magazine than they spend online, there are still over 7,300 print consumer magazines published in the United States (as of 2019), which is up from the previous year.

There are also magazines for which there are specialty categories of every kind. This allows you to target any of hundreds of special-interest groups. Another advantage of magazines, especially monthlies, is that they have a longer shelf life; they're often browsed through for weeks or months after publication and also often have pass-along readership. So your ad might have an audience for up to six months after its initial insertion. Of course, an effective campaign requires multiple insertions. After all, readers can't be expected to see and recall every ad in each issue, and smaller space ads may require even higher frequency than larger ads to get noticed over time.

Researchers have found the following about magazine ads:

- Full-page ads may attract about 70 percent more readers than fractional-page ads.
- Photographs or illustrations dramatically increase an ad's power to draw readers.
- Many successful ads use photographs unrelated to the subject matter.
- It's crucial to maintain a balance between the space devoted to photos or illustrations and copy.
- There must be attention-grabbing text to draw readers' attention, which is crucial for advertising success.

When planning advertising in any print medium, search for the publication online and click on their advertising pages. If you don't find rates or other information that you need, contact the publication, and ask for a media kit. This contains rate information for various sizes of ads as well as demographic information about the publication's readership—age, income, and other details—to help you decide if this is where your buyers are. The media kit also indicates specifications for the format in which you'll have to deliver your ad to the publication.

One thing to keep in mind is that unlike newspapers, magazines have longer lead times. This means that if you're advertising your end-of-year holiday items, you'll probably need to have the ad in their hands in August or September for the December publication. Plan ahead for magazine ads. Also, because you cannot make changes unless you're on the publication's digital version, make sure your ad will be timely when it comes out, then double and triple check that the wording and photographs are exactly as you want them to appear.

Magazine rates vary dramatically based on circulation, ad size, placement in the magazine, and if you are doing a full-color ad. Smaller local magazines are far more affordable than major publications like *AARP* magazine, with rates that can make a new business owner fall off their chair. In fact, WebFX cites an average national magazine advertising cost of $250,000 to run a single full-page ad, plus anywhere from $500 to $397,800 in setup costs to design the ad. This means you may have better luck with smaller, niche magazines.

TIP

The most persuasive words in advertising? Yale University's psychology department discovered that these 14 words are the most powerful, especially when trying to sell or persuade: Free, Now, Easy, Best, New, Save, Safe/Safety, Prove, Discover, Guarantee, Health, Results, and You.

Radio and TV Advertising

Many entrepreneurs believe that TV and radio advertising are beyond their means. But while advertising nationally on commercial network TV may be too costly for many entrepreneurs, advertising on local stations and especially on local cable channels can be surprisingly affordable. The key is to have a clear understanding of your target audience and what they watch or listen to so the money is well spent. "A lot of advertising decisions are made more from the heart than from the head," says William K. Witcher, author of *You Can Spend Less and Sell More*, the classic guide to low-cost advertising. Witcher warns entrepreneurs not to get so swept up in the idea of advertising on TV or radio that they neglect to do the necessary research.

Sitting down and coming up with a well-thought-out advertising plan is crucial, Witcher says. "Don't feel that you can simply throw a bunch of dollars into the advertising mill and create miracles."

Planning is essential if you're approaching broadcast advertising for the first time. Experts suggest entrepreneurs take the following steps before diving in:

- *Use the target audience description from your marketing plan as the basis for your broadcast buy.* Steer clear of any media or programming that doesn't help you reach your audience with as little waste as possible. Be logical in your approach. For example, if your product or service is purchased by women in the 18-to-35-age range, look for the type of programming they watch and when such programs are on.
- *Set a rough budget for broadcast advertising.* Come up with an amount that won't strain your business but will allow you to give broadcast advertising a good try. Many stations suggest running ads for at least three months. Look online for local cable networks or channels and see what they offer regarding rates. Then set your budget for several ads per month. If your commercials are not drawing enough business, perhaps you are better scheduling them for a different time of day. The rates for radio time will vary depending on the size of the market, the station's penetration, and the audience of the shows on which you want to advertise.

SAVE

Considering advertising on cable? Look into a "cable co-op," where several companies collaborate on an ad package that promotes all their services or products.

- *Visit the websites of TV and radio stations in your area and gather whatever information they provide on advertising.* Then email or call to arrange to have a sales representative speak with you. Do your homework first—learn about what is on the station and when. Then ask the sales representative for a list of available spots that air during hours that reach your target audience.

- *Talk to other businesspeople in your area about their experiences with broadcast advertising.* While salespeople from TV and radio stations can be helpful, they are, after all, trying to sell you something. It is your responsibility to be a smart consumer.
- *Ask about the "audience delivery" of the available spots.* Using a published guide (Nielsen), ask the salesperson to help you calculate the CPM (cost per thousand) of reaching your target audience. Remember, you are buying an audience, not just time on a show, and you can calculate exactly how much it's going to cost you to reach each member of that audience.
- *Inquire about the production of your commercial.* Fortunately, major cable companies are now offering production assistance to small-business owners with lower rates than in the past, as they are trying to compete with digital advertising. Some independent TV stations will offer low-cost or free production if you enter into an agreement to advertise for several months. With a similar contract, some radio stations will provide a well-known personality to be the "voice" of your business at no extra cost. However, for multi-voice, high-production value spots, you'll want to enlist an outside production company. That could cost you thousands of dollars depending on how complex your spot is. Hint: In the beginning, think simple. In fact, for radio, you can have ad copy that is read by the on-air personality.

The Small Stuff

Should you use your limited advertising budget to create larger, more visible ads that restrict you to advertising less frequently or place smaller, less visible ads that you can afford to run more frequently?

The answer: smaller ads more frequently. The reason is that most people—even those who are likely candidates for your product—typically don't respond to ads the first time they see them. Prospects may have to notice an ad several times and develop a level of comfort with it (especially if the product or service is new to them) before they take action. The more often prospects see your ad, the more comfortable they'll become and the better the chance they'll respond to it. Of course, if your ad is too small, it may not be seen at all, so be sure to pick an ad size that allows you to shine and still maintain a frequency you can afford. Unlike print, where the size of the ad can make a difference, for TV or radio the length of the ad will factor into the cost to produce it and to buy advertising time. If you can get your message across in a 15- or 30-second spot, by all means do so. The truth is, in today's short attention-span world, nobody wants to sit through minute-long commercials, most of which are not about the benefits of the product or service. Short, entertaining commercials can make a long impression, and that's your goal. Watch the many Geico commercials—they are short, funny, and promote saving time and money. "In Just 15 Minutes, You Could Save $500 or More On Car Insurance."

- *Compare the various proposals.* Look at the offers then negotiate the most attractive deal based on which outlet offers the most cost-effective way of reaching your audience. Buying time well in advance can help lower the cost. Keep in mind that the published rates offered by TV and radio stations are usually negotiable. Generally, rates vary widely during the first quarter of the year and sometimes during the third quarter or late in the fourth quarter, traditionally slow seasons for many businesses; salespeople trying to hit their numbers are more likely to negotiate during these times. But expect to pay full rates during the rest of the year or during popular shows or prime time.

TIP

Get your ad on the radio—for free—by bartering your products or services for airtime. Called trade-out, this practice is common. Radio stations need everything from janitorial services and graphic designers to products they can give away as on-air prizes, so whatever you sell, you're likely to find a ready market.

Getting Help

Once you've gone through all these steps, you should have a good idea what is involved in broadcast advertising. But learning to be a smart consumer in the TV and radio market isn't always easy. If you're worried about making the right choice on your own, consider hiring a consultant or an advertising agency to guide you.

When approaching radio stations, it's important to learn their demographics and look at how closely they match your target market. Sorting out demographics is one area where hiring an ad agency or consultant can help. Every radio station says they are number one in a certain time spot or with a certain audience, so it helps to have an insider on your team.

But don't jump to hire someone before doing your online research. So much information is at your fingertips, so wait until you really need an expert, and not someone who will charge you to give you the facts and figures that are readily available online.

Microtargeting

Radio can be a good option if you only need to reach a small geographic area, such as a single city or town. Another option that can help an advertiser pinpoint a small geographic area is local cable TV. With networks featuring all-news, sports, music, weather, and other specialized topics, cable lets you microtarget the groups that fit your customer profile. Plus, cable TV allows you to reach your target audience in specific towns without wasting money reaching out to viewers who are too far away to use your products or services. Major cable system providers, such as Comcast, Verizon Fios, and Spectrum, allow you to buy advertising on cable programming within geographic zones that can be as small as five miles or in multiple zones to reach an entire major metropolitan area. It's easy to target both geographically and based on the special viewing interests of your audience.

WARNING

Don't wait to market. Fight the tendency to pay too little attention to your customers and resist marketing until you're in trouble. Market when times are good, and you're more likely to keep the good times rolling.

Other examples of TV ad placement might include a business owner looking to reach knowledgeable, politically minded members of the community by advertising on CNN. A sporting goods store might make a big splash by advertising locally during an ESPN sporting event.

But what if you want to target prospects beyond your local broadcast area? If you are selling to a national audience, you can still certainly use cable TV and sometimes radio to achieve your goals. Rather than advertise on your local cable TV provider, for example, you could go directly to national cable networks— from HGTV to ESPN2—and negotiate for a spot schedule on programs that are targeted to your audience.

Today, there are more options than ever to reach national audiences using radio advertising. Thousands of radio stations now simulcast on the internet, and there are networks of internet-only radio stations to suit every breed of listener. If your startup is well-capitalized and you can budget at least $2,500 for a national radio campaign as part of your media mix, you can reach an affluent audience online.

Right Place, Right Time

Today, marketing messages can go anywhere and everywhere people go, thanks to out-of-home advertising. You can reach boaters with advertising at marinas, golfers out on the links with signage on hospitality carts, or health-conscious consumers while they exercise at their local gyms.

Traditional out-of-home advertising encompasses billboards—including today's ubiquitous LED boards on which messages can be changed frequently, even based on the time of day—and transit advertising, from the sides of buses to subway posters and taxi-rooftop ads.

Then there's the out-of-home alternative, generally called place-based advertising. This is where things really get interesting. The "street furniture" category includes bicycle-rack displays and posters on bus shelters, and trash receptacles. Other place-based media include newsstand, convenience store, and shopping mall displays and restaurant menus. You can even try placing posters above diaper-changing stations or in college campus laundry rooms. Your choices and locations are virtually endless.

Follow these three rules for picking the right out-of-home advertising opportunity for your business:

- *Rule one.* The advertising must reach a high percentage of your best prospects. For example, a poster on a bus shelter at a busy intersection can boost sales for a nearby retailer if it is seen often enough by most of the store's customers and prospects.
- *Rule two.* The place-based ad must be in an appropriate venue. The posters you find in the restrooms of popular bars and restaurants typically carry ads for other entertainment-oriented businesses because their messages are compatible with the venue.

- *Rule three.* Your ad must reach prospects at the right time. From billboards promoting business services directed at commuters on their way to work to posters for beauty products in neighborhood hair salons, out-of-home advertising should target your prospects at the time when they'll be most receptive to your message. For example, if you open a terrific takeout food restaurant, perhaps a great place to put your advertising would be across from the train station so that people coming home from work can pick up your food on their way home.

Product Placement

For visual media, product placement (aka embedded marketing) can mean anything from a stage prop with your name on it at the local theater to having a character carrying a shopping bag from your store on a TV show. While you may not have been able to afford to have your Starbucks coffee cup accidentally appear in an episode of *Game of Thrones*, you can place your coffee cups (if that's what you sell) on local talk shows. Yes, you can get a lot of mileage from having your product on TV or even in a film. It worked when UTZ Chips were the chips of choice on *The Office*, and in the classic Spielberg film *E.T.* in which our extraterrestrial friend took a liking to Reese's Pieces.

Local TV studios or production companies can let you know who handles marketing, and while some stations (shows) will ditch the idea of product placement immediately, others will not. To know which shows to approach, keep an eye on TV show credits that say such and such item was furnished by xyz company. For more information, you might start by checking out the Association of Entertainment Marketing Professionals (erma.org) and poking around a bit. That way, the next time someone reaches for a buzzsaw in a horror movie, it could be one of your buzzsaws.

Traditional Radio and Streaming Radio: Still Going Strong

According to Nielsen's "Audio Today 2023" AM/FM radio reaches 91% of U.S. adults each month.Internet radio is also generating attention with nearly 80 percent of internet radio listeners tuning in while they're at work. Therefore, when your spot plays, your prospects are just one click away from your website. In addition to running audio advertising, it's often possible to place online ads your prospects will see while listening.

Among several advantages to radio advertising are the low cost of making a commercial (as mentioned earlier) and the low cost of buying time—typically lower than TV or magazines. Radio also crosses over several technologies and stays with the trends. What that means is that you can reach your customers through their laptop, smartphone, iPad, or basic car radio. In other words, radio travels with your customers, and if you're advertising, your ad is traveling right along with them.

The challenge is to book the best stations that can reach your audience in sufficient numbers to produce results. If you want to search for radio stations in your general vicinity, go to radio-locator.com, which features over 17,700 radio stations' web pages and over 12,700 stations' audio streams from the United States and around the world.

TIP

Don't forget to consider advertising on podcasts. According to Demand-Sage.com, as of 2023 there are 464.7 million podcast listeners globally. This number is predicted to reach 504.9 million by 2024. Find a podcast that attracts your target audience and contact them to find out their advertising rates.

Direct Mail

Direct mail encompasses a wide variety of marketing materials, including brochures, catalogs, postcards, newsletters, and sales letters. For years, major corporations relied heavily on direct-mail advertising as one of the most effective and profitable ways to reach out to new and existing clients.

In recent years, however, direct mail has fallen off because of the immense popularity of digital marketing. However, it is not dead. In fact, many companies are using it in conjunction with their digital marketing campaigns. The advantages of direct mail are that you can target a niche audience, provide detailed information, highlight a featured sale or event you are planning, and put something physically in the hands of your customers, who receive far less actual mail today than ever before—hence you are going against the grain. Even if your audience tosses it, you have a better chance of having it read than you do as one of 100 emails in their inbox. They can also keep it around, meaning they are keeping a reminder of your business in their kitchen or wherever they save it. You can easily track the response rate by including a coupon, which they can bring in or send in.

TIP

Apparently, according to research, larger (oversized) envelopes get a better response rate (5 percent) as opposed to postcards (4.25 percent). Of course, large envelopes can be harder to get into small mailboxes, so make sure it is easy to fold (if necessary) without ruining the design.

Of course, on the flip side, you need to generate or buy a mailing list, have the piece designed and then send it out, which can be costly. Additionally, response rates are typically low, meaning you'll have to send and spend a lot to get some traction. It's also important to do the math to determine if the time and money are worth the return rate, which varies from 2 to 6 percent, depending on where you look or who you ask. Yet, according to the Direct Marketing Association, the average response rate for direct mail house lists is between 5 and 9 percent. More costly or more complicated products can be substantially less.

Unlike other forms of advertising, in which you're never sure just who is getting your message, direct mail lets you communicate one-on-one with your target audience. That allows you to control who receives your message, when it is delivered, what is in the envelope, and how many people you reach.

To create an effective direct-mail campaign, start by getting your name on as many mailing lists as possible. Junk mail isn't junk when you're trying to learn about direct mail. Obtain free information every chance you get, especially from companies that offer products or services similar to yours. Take note of your reaction to each piece of mail, and save the ones that communicate most effectively, whether they come from large or small companies.

The most effective direct-mail inserts often use keywords and colors. Make sure the colors you use promote the appropriate image. Neon colors, for example, can attract attention for party-planner or gift basket businesses. On the other hand, ivory and gray are usually the colors of choice for lawyers, financial planners, and other business services.

To involve the reader in the ordering process, many mailers enclose "yes" or "no" stickers to place on the order form. Companies such as Publishers Clearing House take this technique further by asking recipients to find hidden stickers throughout the mailing and stick them on the sweepstakes entry. It also asks customers to choose their prizes, which gets them even more involved.

Using Technology
No, direct mail and technology are not diametrically opposed. James Joyner, of Joyner Technologies, explains that "technology

has sharpened the direct mail process to provide great results." So where does technology come into play? Joyner says one of the disadvantages of direct mail is the time it takes to move a campaign from conception to completion. Add to that, a higher price tag and a need for manpower. "Technology, however, has made direct mail easier to execute and more affordable than ever," explains Joyner, referring to the way in which direct mail has gone digital. "It lets you digitize the direct mail marketing process, and when done correctly and with the right technological integrations, direct mail marketing can create a more memorable experience for your ideal customer."

Joyner also points to PostcardMania (a $60 million marketing firm that specializes in direct mail) as an example of direct mail fusing with technology. PostcardMania works with companies to take data from their CRM or website and use it to send targeted postcards to their marketing pipeline based on specific triggers, like dates or seasons. Such integration allows business owners to automatically send direct mail in volume, putting an end to what is often a lengthy setup process. Businesses can also benefit from more accurate data, thanks to technology and barcodes that enable direct marketing pieces to be integrated into a company's marketing campaign. The bottom line is technology can help create, store, and disseminate more polished direct-mail pieces than ever.

For more information on direct mail, visit the Association of National Advertisers (ANA), formerly the Direct Marketing Association, at ana.net. It is the national trade organization for direct marketers. You can also check out *Chief Marketer*, an online and print publication with resources online at chiefmarketer.com/channel/direct-marketing-print/.

Read It, Read It

Even the best-written direct-mail campaign won't be effective if your mailer doesn't show up at your intended recipients' doors. Or what if they arrive only to be tossed in the trash?

There are some simple things you can do to increase the chances that your sale pieces arrive at the right place and get opened.

- *Make sure your list is good.* The key element to getting your mail delivered is to make sure you start with an accurate, updated mailing list that you get from your actual audience. This is also instrumental in making sure that you get your mail opened by your target audience. If your list doesn't target the people most likely to respond to your offer, it can be useless.
- *Make them want to read.* Now you want your recipient to open your mailer and look through it. Be sure you are using the right format that will most appeal to your prospects. Every market niche has its own qualities, and you need to find out and employ the format that works best for yours. Find out who the most successful marketers are in your niche and follow what they're doing.

Mailing Lists

No matter what type of direct mail you send out, you'll need a mailing list. The basic way to build a mailing list is by capturing name and address information for everyone who buys or shows interest in your product. If you sell by mail, you'll already have this information. If not, you can get it off customers' checks. Hold a drawing and ask customers to fill out an entry card or drop their business cards in a bowl. Or if you're a retailer, simply put a mailing list book next to your cash register where customers can sign up to receive mailers and advance notices of sales. One of the best ways to build a mailing list is to compile a database using the leads generated by your other forms of advertising. The key is to build a list that is generated using the permission of the prospects.

The list you develop using your own customers' names is called your house list. Of course, when you're starting out, your house list is likely to be skimpy. To augment it, one way to go is to rent a mailing list. There are two ways to rent a mailing list: approaching the company you want to rent from directly or using a list broker. Keep in mind, however, that renting or buying a mailing list doesn't often bode well, for several reasons. First, most recipients are unaware that they are on the list, so they see your mailing as unsolicited or "junk," hence the term junk mail. This can sour them from doing business with you. Second, as noted with TV and radio, advertising is most effective when you do it often. In this case, sending unwanted mail often will further distance your customer from you. Third, it is not always timely because it takes time to produce the materials and get them to the folks on the mailing list. This can also take a lot of time that you or your employees could have spent doing something more productive. And finally, let's not forget that most direct mailings are tossed in the garbage, or elsewhere, which means you are leading to the buildup of trash, which remains a major environmental concern.

If you cannot build your own list of customers, because you don't have time or you are a new business, you are probably better off waiting and compiling one as you build your customer base. If, however, you are determined to buy or rent a mailing list, googling mailing list brokers is an option. They know all the lists available and can advise you on what type of list would work best for your business. Many can also custom-create lists based on your requirements. The ANA can also refer you to brokers. Mailing lists for 1,000 consumer names and addresses can cost up to $200, and for businesses, $350. Keep in mind that lists are commonly not updated, meaning that you will find names of people who have moved or are deceased.

A list will typically be provided in an electronic format or on pre-printed mailing labels and sent directly to the vendor you want to do the final mailing. Consider using a mailing house.

Mailing houses have the equipment to professionally cut and apply preprinted labels or to download electronic files and rapidly create and affix labels by the thousands to your envelopes. A large mailing house can also personalize and print your letter and envelope, handle the folding and insertion, and do everything else associated with assembling your direct-mail package. Depending on the level of service you need, rates may range from a few hundred to several thousand dollars for a 5,000-piece mailing.

SAVE
If you have an in-house (organically created) mailing list, keep it up-to-date by cleaning it regularly. To do this, send out mailers with the notation "Address Correction Requested." The post office won't charge you for sending you the new addresses of your customers when the cards are returned.

Brochures
For many businesses, especially service companies, a brochure is a building block of all marketing materials. Today, it might be considered a tangible version of your website, with a similar design and information. A brochure is an information piece that doubles as an image maker. A brochure not only describes the benefits of your product or service, but it also conveys your legitimacy and professionalism. It can provide your customers with a takeaway from your business.

The good news is that a brochure doesn't have to be expensive. It can be as simple as a piece of folded paper—the same piece of letter-sized paper that would otherwise be a flier. By folding it twice, as you would a letter, then turning it upright so it opens like a book, you have the basis for a brochure.

The magic of the brochure format is that it allows for a more dramatic presentation of the material than does a flier, and it is usually on higher-quality paper. Think of your brochure cover as the stage curtain, creating anticipation of the excitement that lies inside. An eye-catching headline on the cover is like the master of ceremonies, piquing the prospect's interest about what's behind the "curtain." Inside, you first need to pay off the promise, or claim, in the cover headline with another headline, then use the remaining space for elaboration.

The principles of writing successful brochures are basically the same as those for writing print ads. However, brochures offer more room than ads, so there is a tendency to get long-winded and wordy. Keep your brochure brief, with enough information to interest readers but not so much repetition that they get bored. Use benefit-laden headlines and subheads, and "explain" your benefits by detailing all your features in the body copy.

TIP

Even if you do most of your business online or over the phone, customers like to see whom they're doing business with. Unless you have good reason not to (and there aren't many!), put your photo on your brochures or mailings. It conveys friendliness and builds confidence in your company.

The overall look of a brochure is the key to making a good impression on prospective customers. Here are some tips to make sure yours is inviting to the eye:

- *Use a fairly large size type for the descriptive copy.* There's no bigger turnoff for a prospect than squinting at tiny printing.
- *Use light-colored paper.* This, too, makes the brochure easier to read.
- *Break up the copy with subheads.* This makes the overall brochure less intimidating to read.

- *Add something visually unexpected.* One idea is to use a striking photo or graphic on the cover.
- *Use the back of your brochure for a "business biography."* This is a good place to talk about how your company got started, how it has succeeded, and where it is today.
- *Always use endorsements.* Include testimonials, industry affiliations, or other credibility-raising elements.
- *Spend a little extra money.* Have your brochure printed on cover stock or quality heavyweight paper because it makes a better impression in a customer's hand.

If you search for "sample brochures" online, you will get many examples from places like Vistaprint or www.gotprint.com, as well as templates and plenty of information about creating your own brochures.

Sales Letters

Whether you send it out solo or as part of a direct-mail package, a sales letter can be one of your most effective marketing tools, allowing you to speak one-on-one to prospects and customers. What makes a good sales letter? There are three key rules:

1. *Start with a hook.* Begin your letter with a provocative thought or idea that hooks readers and makes them want to keep reading.
2. *Give them the facts fast.* Quickly list the top two or three benefits of doing business with your company.
3. *End persuasively.* Close the letter with a strong argument that compels readers to respond.

How long should a sales letter be? The standard answer is "long enough to do the job." And yes, it takes longer to persuade a prospective customer to buy than to merely get him to inquire further. But in today's high-tech age, people become impatient with anything that takes much longer than an eye blink to read. Does this mean the sales letter is dying out? No; people will still read sales letters. However, they don't like it when you make them work at it—so keep it lean and mean.

Equal in importance to your message (some would say more important) is the look of your letter. It should be visually inviting. If it's crammed with words, readers will get a negative impression.

To have the best chance of being read, your letter should be open and airy-looking with short paragraphs—including some that are one sentence or even one word long. (A one-word paragraph? Here's how: Write something like "I have one word for suppliers who say they can't offer you a one-year guarantee." Follow that with a one-word paragraph such as "Baloney!" or any similar word. It is a real attention-getter.)

Search for sample sales letters online and you will find many to look at, including those for new prospects and existing customers. Use them as a guide when you write your own.

Strip your sales message down to the essentials so readers can breeze through it. This may mean hacking out words and phrases you have slaved over. But each extra bit you take out increases your chances of getting a response.

Finally, be sure to use "you." This is a good rule of thumb in any form of advertising but especially in a sales letter, where you are, in a sense, talking to the prospect face-to-face. Always talk about your product or service in terms of its benefit to the reader, such as "You'll save time," or "You'll save money." Sounds obvious, but it's easy to lapse into the impersonal "we" mode, as in "We offer our customers discounts of more than 50 percent."

TIP

Trial sizes and sampling work: Have employees pass out product samples in front of your store; if you provide a service, offer a free trial period or consultation.

Postcards

The humble postcard has the power to beat all other direct-marketing formats when it comes to generating sales leads. Why is the postcard so effective? It's much less costly to prepare and mail than other direct-mail efforts, but that's not its greatest strength. It can be mailed out practically overnight, but that's not its greatest strength, either.

The real power of a postcard is that it takes only a flip of the wrist for recipients to get your message. They read their name on it, then flip it over to see what's on the other side. Simple, but incredibly powerful. Why? Because a huge percentage of direct mail never gets opened. That's the keyword "opened." A postcard never has to overcome that obstacle.

More than letters, postcards convey a sense of urgency, making them an ideal way to notify customers of a limited-time offer or special sale.

What's an even better way for companies to get attention in the nanosecond of time it takes for the recipient to turn a postcard over? Businesses can create a catchy nickname to use for the purposes of advertising. Nicknames can work for many types of service businesses. For example:

- For a wedding planner: The Marriage Maestro
- For an auto mechanic: The Car Medic
- For a party-planning service: The Party Smarty
- For a carpenter: The Wood Wizard

You get the idea. Next, add an eye-catching graphic on the front of the postcard, along with a provocative headline or teaser that conveys the company's benefit.

TIP

It's easy to get caught up in marketing campaigns that bring sales from new customers yet overlook the importance of retaining existing customers. It's less expensive to upsell an old customer than to win a new one, so you need to strike a balance between acquisition and retention tactics, such as loyalty programs. This is a good reason to send reminder emails and/or postcards.

"A life spent making mistakes is not only more honorable but more useful than a life spent doing nothing."

—George Bernard Shaw

Fliers

A hybrid of the postcard and brochure, fliers give you more room to get your message across than a postcard but are cheaper (and easier to design) than a brochure.

Fliers are ideal for certain situations, such as for posting on a bulletin board or handing out at an event. They are also a good tool to enclose with a sales letter if, for example, you want to notify recipients about a short-term sale or upcoming special event.

Because fliers' primary benefit is that they convey information quickly, make sure yours is easy to read and stands out. Try bright colors to grab the viewer's eye, and use large type so information can be seen from a distance. Keep type brief and to the point. A crowded flier won't get anyone's attention.

Don't use fliers as your only direct-mail tool, or you could come off looking amateurish.

Catalogs

Recently thought to be on the same road to extinction as the dodo bird, the Edsel, and the eight-track tape player, printed catalogs aren't quite dead. In fact, researchers say they are having a resurgence.

According to the *Harvard Business Review* (HRB), catalog mailings have been steadily on the rise since 2015, and customers are surprisingly enthusiastic about receiving them. In an article from early 2020, HRB noted that response rates from catalogs increased by 170 percent between 2004 and 2018, and there's no indication that they have been losing ground since. In 2023, catalogs as a direct mail strategy are experiencing a big resurgence. Most likely this is a result of several things, like being able to precisely target your audience and personalize the content.

Many major brands, including online giants like Amazon and Wayfair, have gone back to the basics, providing printed catalogs that allow customers to browse the pages. Part of the appeal is that catalogs make the products more real, vivid, and memorable. Some people still enjoy holding the catalog and browsing the pages. It's a more tactile experience than looking at the screen, where so many people spend the bulk of their time. Today's catalogs present imagery, settings, and wording that make the products more enticing, elegant, and provocative than the usual splash of merchandise on a website.

Research has also shown that catalogs have a stronger influence on purchase decisions than websites or TV commercials. The ANA points out that "while online marketing is passive, direct mail is active. Direct mailings are proactive and tactile—demanding the recipient to do something with it."

If you're going to put together a catalog, make sure to set aside a significant budget and review catalogs from your competitors. Then follow these five tips to ensure your catalog descriptions are brief, which will help make your catalog a success.

1. *Keep it simple.* Don't try to reinvent the wheel. Catalogs look the way they do for a reason. Almost every format you can imagine has been tested numerous times, and those you see most often are the most effective. Choose one of the most common sizes, such as 48 or 64 pages, because catalog

publishers typically work with multiples of 8.

2. *Borrow from the best.* The surest way to plot your catalog layout is to study other catalogs—at least 20. You'll then have a collection of the best ideas from the best designers and copywriters money can buy. Study the catalogs, and note any useful ideas.

3. *Choose a production route.* With the abundance of high-quality desktop publishing programs, chances are you can easily create your own camera-ready catalog design. Microsoft Publisher, for example, includes a design "wizard" that shows you how to easily lay out your catalog pages. The real challenge is to create hardworking copy that's professional, clean, and motivates customers to purchase the featured products. If you're up to the task, you can save considerable production costs by completing this step on your own. If not, you should look for a professional design team that's experienced in catalog production. Or you may want to hire a copywriter to review your initial efforts and improve them before printing your catalog. After all, with the cost of printing, postage, and rental lists, sending a poorly produced piece is a costly mistake.

WARNING
Don't launch a direct-mail campaign (especially a catalog) until you're sure you can handle the orders you might receive. If fulfillment systems aren't in place and orders don't get sent out, you'll lose credibility—and future business.

4. *Find the perfect printer.* Shop around—you'll be amazed at the range of prices printers will quote you for the same job. If you live in a small town, call large printers in nearby metropolitan areas because they often offer substantial

savings and give quotes over the phone. And don't overlook the internet when it comes to shopping for the best printer. Some of the country's largest printers have made it easy to order online, and this is where you may find the most attractive pricing. You can email them your artwork and often receive a free or very low-cost sample before you commit to buying in bulk. It's a good idea to get at least three bids on any print job you plan to run, and get six or more on a big one, typically over 1,000 items. You might be able to barter for a discounted price with a local printer if the businesses owner needs or wants your services.

Printers will want to know the physical dimensions of your catalog, whether it will be in four-color, the number of pages to be printed, the kind of paper you want, and the number of catalogs you plan to order. The more catalogs you print, the cheaper your cost per unit.

Gifts That Keep on Giving

Do you offer customers gift certificates or gift cards? Many entrepreneurs don't, not realizing how this can boost sales. Here are some suggestions to make the most of this sales tool and prevent fraud:

- *Don't buy generic gift certificates from stationery or office supply stores.* These can easily be duplicated. Invest in custom-designed certificates.
- *Avoid cash refunds.* State on the certificate that if more than $5 in change is due, it will be issued in the form of another gift certificate.
- *Keep a log.* Record the number, date of sale, and dollar amount of each gift certificate sold. Be sure to note when the certificate is redeemed.
- *Use security features like an embossed logo or watermark to prevent photocopying.*
- *Go online with third-party discount services like Groupon,* which introduce customers to your product by offering a discount.

Properly used, certificates are like money in the bank for your business because customers often don't redeem them until months after they're purchased. Or consider plastic gift cards or e-cards that are only activated upon purchase.

5. *Put it all together.* You can spend tens of thousands of dollars on a mail-order catalog, but if you do as much as you can yourself, you won't have to. Today's technology makes catalog production and layout simpler than ever.

Of course, the real key to catalog success doesn't lie exclusively in technology—it's understanding your customers. Show them why they should buy from you and no one else.

Need more help? The ANA can refer you to catalog consultants in your area.

TIP

Consider a loyalty program for customers. It could be in the form of a punch card, such as buy a certain number of items of products and receive a discount or free item or have nine haircuts and your tenth is free. You can also offer a loyalty card, similar to those found at local grocery stores. These customers get discounts or accumulate points for a discount or free item.

Similarly, you can offer discount cards for students who are often pressed for cash and for seniors who may also be looking to save money. Many stores today simply offer senior days, with discounts to anyone over 62 or 65.

Newsletters

Publishing a company newsletter is a great way to get the word out about your business, and keep customers coming back. While most business owners have changed from printed newsletters to electronic newsletters (enewsletters), which are cheaper to make and sent for free via email, there are still some target audiences, such as seniors, that respond best to old-fashioned snail mail. If your newsletter becomes well-known for interesting, relatable, valuable content, your readers will spend time reading it.

Premium Prospects

Whether you call them premiums or advertising specialties, gifts are a marketing tool that works with all demographic groups. Actually, they are promotional items and you can usually buy them in bulk, with your company name on them, for a good rate. Studies show that 40 percent of people remember an advertiser's name up to six months after receiving a promotional product as a gift.

Premiums carrying your company name, logo, or message can be used to generate leads, build name awareness, thank customers, increase store traffic, introduce new products, motivate customers, and create a subconscious obligation to buy. Premiums can be used at trade shows, open houses, special events and grand openings, and in direct-mail pieces.

Classic premiums include T-shirts, baseball caps, jackets, headbands, writing instruments, desk and office accessories, scratch pads, stress balls, sports bottles, tote bags, umbrellas, and mugs. Mouse pads and small high-tech devices are some of the more recent premiums gaining popularity.

How to make a premium work for you? Research it first. Make sure the item is matched with your target audience. Also make sure the item is good quality. A cheap premium that breaks or doesn't work makes a negative impression—just the opposite of what you want.

When choosing a premium, ask five questions:

1.   How many people do I want to reach?

2. How much money do I have to spend?
3. What message do I want to print?
4. What gift will be most useful to my prospects?
5. Is this gift unique and desirable? Would I want it?

You can find plenty of choices, plus prices, by searching "promotional products" online.

While the gift is being offered, focus your marketing and advertising efforts on it. There's no more powerful word in advertising than "free," so put the power of freebies, albeit small ones, to work for you.

TIP

Although newsletters give you room for lengthier articles, keep the bulk of your newsletter limited to short pieces, so they are scannable. You want lots of different items in the hope of providing something interesting to every reader. Enewsletters should also be succinct. However, because it's just a matter of scrolling or not, you can use the added room to include a bunch of promotions at the bottom. People can then scroll or not as they see fit. In other words, you've got nothing to lose.

Enewsletters should focus on what is of interest to your readers. The businesses that benefit most from newsletters/enewsletters are those that have to educate customers about the advantages of using their product or service and include some interesting tidbits, in general about the type of items they sell or services they provide. Therefore, if you own a sporting goods store and you sell tennis racquets, write about some of the best racquets to come along (that you sell) and something about the sport now or historically. A little general reporting on what's going on in your industry can be of interest to your audience. If you are in the landscaping business, for example, you might write about great ideas for the garden as spring approaches or how to nurse your garden through the cold months if winter is coming. Your newsletter doesn't have to be all information. Including a coupon, a special offer, or other call to action helps get people to buy. Also, always give upcoming sales or promotions a prominent place in your newsletter. And finally, avoid talking about the inner workings of your business. While it's terrific that Jennifer got a promotion and you've just hired a new sales manager, outside of your store, office, or warehouse, nobody cares. Headlines like "Mark Smith Promoted to National Head of Toiletries" will land your newspaper in the trash can or get your newsletter immediately deleted.

For many businesses, newsletters and enewsletters have given way to blogs, which are shorter, easy to write, and quick to disseminate.

Package Deal

While direct mail can mean everything from a postcard to a catalog, many business owners get the best response from sending out a direct-mail "package." In addition to the sales letter and brochure (see the "Sales Letters" and "Brochures" sections earlier in this chapter), this typically includes three other elements:

1. *The outside envelope.* There are three schools of thought on this. One school swears that "teaser" copy on the envelope can get recipients to open it. On the other hand, some people throw away anything that looks like junk mail. The opposite strategy is to trick readers into opening your mail by sending direct mail that looks like personal letters. Most people, however, will be less than happy to be tricked into opening something that they thought was "important." The one that does work is having a well-designed envelope featuring something of interest to your audience, such as flowers for garden lovers or boats for boating enthusiasts.
2. *A response form.* The form should be easy to fill out. Be sure to include your phone number and email address in case the prospect wants to ask a question or place an order on your website or by phone.

3.   *A reply envelope.* Enclosing postage-paid reply envelopes helps get orders. Even if you can't afford postage-paid envelopes, include a pre-addressed reply envelope.

Consider giving people the option to go online to fill out a form or ask questions.

When creating your newsletter, keep your writing style simple, and make sure you get help proofreading if your skills aren't up to snuff, or you simply want another pair of eyes to look at it. A newsletter full of typos or grammatical errors doesn't bode well for business.

Newsletters can be monthly, semimonthly, or quarterly, depending on your budget, how much time you have, and the pace of your industry. Quarterly publications are generally sufficient to get your name in front of customers, then increase the frequency if needed. The key is to be consistent, so don't take on more than you can handle.

FYI

It's advantageous to integrate your newsletter with your social media platforms. For an enewsletter, it's simply a link (or several), or in print, you just include your business handle for Twitter or Instagram, or your link to Facebook and/or LinkedIn. See which of these or other social media sites are the most popular with your demographic.

Many smartphone users habitually enter their location using these apps. Integrating your direct-mail campaign with your online marketing efforts can also have a successful halo effect that works both ways by amplifying your message; a direct-mail campaign heightens awareness and online reinforcement reminds customers they're already familiar with your company when they're close by or in need of your service or product.

Classified Ads

Believe it or not, classified ads (in print or online) can still get you noticed, even in the age of social media. Classified ads are a smart way to reach prospects who are looking for—and are prepared to buy—what you sell. And because they demand neither the eye-catching design of a display ad nor the clever wording of a direct-mail campaign, almost anyone can write them.

What should your ad say? The News Media Alliance recommends listing your product or service's main benefit. Does it make people money? Improve their self-image? Use a catchy statement, such as "Feel Good Now!" to create an impact. Not every reader is looking for the same benefit, so list as many as you can afford. The more readers know about your business, the more they'll trust you.

Experts also recommend using white space to make your classified ad stand out from the competition. White space works especially well in newspapers, which sell ads for pennies a word or by the line. Place just a few words in each line—the first line listing a benefit, the second the name of your company, the third your address, or online address. Classifieds are a case where the saying "less is more" holds true.

These brief ads work best when they offer a commonly sold product or service, such as tax preparation or catering. Listing the benefits of each isn't essential because the public knows what to expect. White space in classifieds is also effective when you offer a catalog or another form of literature describing your product. In this case, you might place the main benefit in an opening line that's designed to grab the reader's attention, and below the benefit list how to send for the information, noting its price, if any. For example, "Play Backgammon Like a Pro" would be a good benefit line in an ad offering free information about a booklet, or even an online course that shows backgammon players how to improve their game.

"The workplace should primarily be an incubator for the human spirit."
—Anita Roddick, founder of The Body Shop

Ads that use white space are less common in magazines because these ads are often far more costly than a typical online or newspaper classified. However, they are often more effective because few other white space ads will be competing for readers' attention.

Before placing your classified ad, contact the publication and ask for a media kit, or download one from the company's website. This should include guidelines that will help you construct your ad and give you tips on choosing the main benefit, consolidating words, or determining whether the tone should be boldly stated or instead employ a conservative description and a list of benefits. Most media kits also list demographic information about the readers—essential information to determining if the publication is right for you.

Finally, repeat your ad as often as possible, as long as it brings in enough money to justify its expense. Repeating ads helps customers gain familiarity with your product or service and helps break down sales resistance. Once the ad stops pulling in new accounts, it's time to develop a new ad. A classified that uses fewer words will cost less to run, so it doesn't have to pull as well to justify itself. But sometimes adding more words can help your sales, too. If people aren't quite getting the point of your ad, try using a few more words to explain. It doesn't hurt to experiment until you find the right balance.

How much profit do you need to make on classifieds? Unless you're running a one-product, one-sale business, you can build a profitable operation through classifieds just by breaking even, or even by coming in a little under the money, because many of those buyers will become your repeat customers.

Let's Make a Deal

Even if your marketing strategy is working well, you may still be looking for ways to boost your sales, drive more traffic, and increase your awareness online. For many small businesses, that means turning to deal websites like Groupon (www.groupon.com) that provide a platform for companies to offer discounts on products and services.

Groupon and other sites make money by charging a fee for advertising and promoting their offers. In most cases, that fee is a percentage of the revenue generated by selling on Groupon. For small businesses, there's one obvious downside: you're offering your product or service at a discount, and the deal site is taking a cut of what the customer pays. On a $100 product, that could mean you only realize, say, $55 in revenue if you offer a $30 discount and the deal site takes a cut of, say, $15. That's why most businesses use such sites in a limited way.

Of course, there are upsides.

For example, many small businesses and entrepreneurs don't have the connections to broaden their audience quickly. Using a discount website to promote limited deals helps expose you to a larger audience and gives you a chance to win over customers.

About 66 percent of companies say they see an increase in sales through deal sites.

Discount sites also offer you a way to promote products when you might have a surplus of inventory you need to pare down—while again exposing new people to your company.

What's more, using a discount deal website can help your business build its reputation. Offering a discount can spur a potential customer to try your company. Deliver a quality product or service when they do, and you're more likely to see repeat business and recommendations from these deal-first customers.

However, you need to be prepared. There have been restaurants and other businesses that were not prepared and found themselves unable to accommodate the increase in customers. As a result, they took a hit to their reputation, and in many cases, even ended up losing money.

Co-Op Advertising

How can small retailers or distributors maintain a high profile without spending lots of money? One answer is co-op advertising.

Co-op advertising is a cooperative advertising effort between suppliers and retailers—such as between a soda company and a convenience store that advertises the company's products.

Both retailers and suppliers benefit: retailers because co-op advertising increases the amount of money they can spend on ads, and suppliers through increased local exposure and better sales.

Although each manufacturer or supplier that uses co-op advertising sets up its own individual program, all co-op programs run on the same basic premise. The retailer or distributor builds a fund (called accrual) based on the number of purchases made from the supplier. Then when the retailer or distributor places ads featuring that supplier's products, the supplier reimburses all or part of the cost of the ad up to the amount accrued.

To start using co-op advertising, begin by asking your suppliers what co-op programs they offer. Follow their rules to be sure you get reimbursed. Some suppliers require that ads feature only their products, not any other supplier's. Others ask that no competing products be included. Though procedures may vary, there are three basic steps to filing a claim for reimbursement. First, show "proof of performance." For print ads, this is just a copy of the ad exactly as it was printed. If you buy TV or radio ads, you'll need a copy of the script with station affidavits of the dates and times aired.

Next, document the cost of the advertising—usually with copies of applicable invoices from the publication or station where you ran the ad. Third, fill out and submit a claim form, which you can get from the supplier.

Other steps to make the most of co-op advertising:

- Keep careful records of how much you have purchased from each supplier.

- If you try something unusual, such as a sales video or a catalog, get prior approval from each vendor before proceeding.
- If you're preparing your own ads, work with an advertising professional to prepare an ad you think will appeal to the manufacturer. Keep in mind the image the manufacturer presents in its own ads.
- Make sure your company's name stands out in the ad. Your goal is not so much to sell the supplier's product but to get customers into your store.
- If there's no established co-op program, pitch your ad campaign to the vendor anyway.
- Expect vendors to help; after all, you're bringing them business. If your vendor doesn't offer advertising co-op money, you should look for another vendor that does.
- Always follow up. Money goes only to those who submit claims.

TIP
Your marketing plan is an ongoing process. Market conditions change. Some of tomorrow's challenges you can predict today, while others you can never anticipate. You should look at your plan at least every three months and on a formal basis every six months. If you aren't on track, why not? Has your thinking changed or has the market thrown you a curve?

Measuring Advertising Effectiveness

Just as important as creating a strong marketing plan is following through on the results. How will you know which ads are working if you don't analyze the results? Keep in mind that there is no one standard way of measuring effective advertising, especially when you're advertising across a range of media. There are, however, some general methods of determining how your ads are doing. You can check the effectiveness of your advertising programs regularly by conducting one or more of the following tests:

- *One basic way to track advertising is by counting.* Online ads can usually be tracked by various analytics. You can monitor how many clicks you are getting, which pages people are looking at, and most significantly, how long they are staying on your site. Google Analytics is popular for tracking ads by providing a variety of data. You can also count coupons redeemed, customers (in a small enterprise) that enter your business, or specific products sold vs. how many were sold in a week or month prior to running your advertising campaign so you have a means of comparison.
- *Train everyone in your company who takes email orders or answers the phone to ask customers where they heard about you.* Create a one-page form with checkboxes so this process is simple to follow and the results are easy to evaluate. Just bear in mind that customers will sometimes get it wrong—they may say they saw you on TV when you don't run a TV campaign. But overall, asking for this information will be valuable.
- *Advertise an item in one ad only.* Don't have any signs or otherwise promote the item in your store or business. Then count the emails, calls, sales, or special requests for that item. If you get emails or calls, you'll know the ad is working.
- *Stop running an ad for a couple of weeks that you regularly run.* See if dropping the ad affects visitors to your website, store traffic, and/or sales.
- *Always check sales results.* This is especially important when you place an ad for the first time.

Checks like these will give you some idea of how your advertising and marketing program is working. Be aware, however, that you can't expect immediate results from an ad. Advertising consistently is important, especially if you run small-space ads, which are less likely to be seen and remembered than larger ads.

Coupon Cutters

If you want to attract and keep customers, you need to offer an incentive. A coupon for a free sample or service, or a discount on your normal prices, can be just the nudge a customer needs to try your new business. Coupons help you achieve many goals: introducing a new product or service, increasing repeat business, beating the competition, and more.

One of the most powerful ways to use coupons is through direct mail. This method is especially good for occasions, such as grand openings or new product/service introductions. How can you make the most of your direct-mail coupon campaign? Keep these tips in mind:

- Coupons can be offered as a "Thank you for buying from us" or a "Stop by and try us" message.
- A coupon can be a single item for a one-shot promotion or used in combination with other offers.
- The value must be substantial enough to make it worthwhile. Better to err on the side of giving too big a discount than to seem cheap.
- Use coupon promotions sparingly. They wear themselves out if overused and customers begin to expect a coupon and might delay purchases until they get one.
- Be clear. State exactly what the offer is, how long it lasts, and the terms of redemption.
- Color-code your coupons if a variety of groups will receive them. For example, if you're mailing to six zip codes, color-code them differently so you know how many were redeemed from each area.

- Make sure everyone in your business knows that you have coupons out there and how to accept them (which includes checking the expiration dates). Having someone on your staff receive a coupon from a customer and then look at the customer like they are from outer space—or even worse—argue with the customer that it must be bogus is bad for business. It does happen.
- If the coupon is for a product, rather than a service, make sure you have enough of that product on hand to meet an increased demand. You will have a lot of unhappy customers if you run out of the item quickly.

You could offer coupons through a postcard mailing, combining an effective direct-mail method with an effective get-them-in-the-door effort. You can also distribute coupons on the internet. Add a registration box to the main page of your website so people can sign up to receive coupons. This way, you can build a permission-based email list of people who want to receive ongoing offers and rewards. Or consider using a web coupon service, which offers coupons online for consumers to download and print out themselves or have a barcode that can be scanned from their smartphones. Valpak (valpak.com) and *Clipper* magazine (clippermagazine.com) are two popular services. You can also offer a coupon to be printed on the back of grocery store customers' receipts—IndoorMedia (indoormedia.com) is the main company that offers this service to advertisers and grocers. The Register Tape Network (rtn.net) is another. Sixty percent of consumers say they actively look for coupons, so whichever route you choose, it can be a worthwhile method for getting people to use or know your business.

"No person can get very far in life working 40 hours a week."
    —J. Willard Marriott, founder of Marriott International Inc.

One study showed that attention to an ad is significantly

impacted by its size—in fact, a 1 percent increase in ad size leads to the same percentage increase in attention.

Check with the ANA regularly for the latest stats on effectiveness, and if you're using online advertising, you should be able to get metrics from your website host or tracking codes attached to your advertisements.

CHAPTER 6

Talking Points

How to Promote Your Business

PAYING FOR ADVERTISING ISN'T THE ONLY WAY to spread the word about your business. In fact, one of the best ways to get your business noticed does not have to cost you a dime. We are talking about public relations.

Public relations is a broad category, spanning everything from press releases and networking at chamber of commerce meetings to sponsoring contests or holding gala special events. This chapter will show you the basics of public relations and give you plenty of ideas to get started. And ideas are what it's all about because when it comes to public relations, you are limited only by your own imagination.

Getting Publicity

Just what is public relations? And how does it differ from advertising? Public relations is the opposite of advertising. In advertising, you pay to have your message placed in a newspaper, TV, or radio spot. In public relations, the article that features your company is not paid for—some marketing and PR professionals refer to it as "earned" media. That is, your business, your persona, or what you're doing is interesting enough that the press is writing about it because it's worthwhile and interesting. Your goal is to have a reporter, journalist, or blogger, write about, talk about, or even film your company because of the information they received from you.

Publicity is more effective than advertising for several reasons. First, publicity can be far more cost-effective than advertising. It can cost you nothing (except for some time) if you are proficient at networking, doing some online research, and writing your own press releases. If, however, you hold corporate events or hire PR firms to handle the job for you, costs can add up.

Like advertising, you should have a public relations plan, or campaign as it's often called, that includes sending out press releases, queries, emails, taking part in community activities, and so forth. Public relations is all about getting the word out to the public, or at least your segment of it, which is your target audience.

Second, publicity can reach a far wider audience than advertising generally does. Sometimes your story might even be picked up by the national media, spreading the word about your business all over the country, and if something about your business (hopefully positive) goes viral on the internet, your story can span the globe. You can also use influencers online and, of course, promote your business (subtly) on social media.

TIP

Find out the lead times for the media in which you want to run your promotional piece. Magazines, for instance, typically work several months in advance, so if you want to get a story about your business in the December issue, you may need to send a press release in June.

Finally, and most importantly, publicity has greater credibility with the public than advertising. Readers feel that if an objective third party—a web content writer, blogger, magazine, newspaper, or radio reporter—is featuring your company or even just quoting you as an authority as part of a larger article on a topic related to your business, you must be doing something worthwhile.

Why do some companies succeed in generating publicity while others don't? It's been proven time and time again that no matter how large or small your business is, the key to securing publicity is identifying your target market and developing a well-thought-out public relations campaign. To get your company noticed, follow these seven steps. You'll notice that many are similar or identical to steps you went through when developing your marketing plan.

1. *Write your positioning statement.* This sums up in a few sentences what makes your business different from the competition.
2. *List your objectives.* What do you hope to achieve for your company through the publicity plan you put into action? List your top five goals in order of priority. Be specific, and always set deadlines. Using a clothing boutique as an example, some goals may be to:
   - Increase your store traffic, which will translate into increased sales.
   - Create a high profile for your store within the community.
3. *Identify your target customers.* Are they male or female? What age range? What are their lifestyles, incomes, and buying habits? Where do they live?
4. *Identify your target media.* List the websites, newspapers, and TV and radio programs in your area that would be appropriate outlets. Make a complete list of the media you want to target, then email or call them, and ask whom you should contact regarding your area of business. Identify the specific assignment editor, writer, blogger, reporter, or producer who covers your area so you can contact them directly. You can research online to find all the above media outlets. Make your own media directory, listing names, emails, addresses, and telephone numbers. Make sure you know the people who write about, or talk about, your industry.

5. *Develop story angles.* Keeping in mind the media you are approaching, make a list of story ideas you can pitch to them. Develop story angles your audience would want to read about, talk about online, or see on TV. Think back to the last story about a company that got your attention. What angle and interest was in that story and others that caught your eye?

If you own a toy store, for example, one angle could be to donate toys to the local hospital's pediatric wing. If you own a clothing store, you could alert the local media to a fashion trend in your area. What's flying out of your store so fast you can't keep it in stock? If it's shirts featuring Winnie the Pooh, you could talk to the media about the return of children's nostalgia. Then arrange for a reporter to speak with some of your customers about why they purchased that particular shirt. Text or email some photos of the shirts.

While a lot of people like to write about themselves, this will only work if you have a compelling and unique story. It's better to write about your business and what makes it unique; are you the first to introduce a service or product into your area? Did your business win a prestigious award? Did your sports memorabilia shop just sell a baseball card for $1.5 million dollars? Was your original clothing line just featured on a major network TV program?

Perhaps your business did something for the community. Did you donate the excess land behind your shop to the town to build a playground for disabled children? Did your company help place 50 stranded or sheltered dogs and cats in good homes?

AHA!

When considering media that can publicize your business, don't forget the "hidden" media in your community. These can include free publications from neighborhood associations, or those for singles, seniors, tourists, local companies' employees, or social or charitable organizations like the Junior League.

6. *Make the pitch.* Put your thoughts on paper, and send them to the editor, blogger, writer, reporter, or producer in a pitch letter (aka query). Start with an interesting fact that relates your business to the target medium's audience. For instance, if you were writing for a magazine aimed at seniors, you could start with "Surveys show that more than half of all women over 50 have not begun saving for retirement." Then lead into your pitch: "As a Certified Financial Planner, I can offer your readers ten tips to start them on the road to a financially comfortable retirement . . ." Then add an example or two. Make your letter no longer than one page; include your cell number (so they can call or text you if they so choose) and email address so the reporter can contact you.

If appropriate, include a press release with your letter, or just email the press release. Be sure to include your positioning statement at the end of any correspondence or press releases you send.

TIP

Sending out publicity photos with your press release or kit? Make them fun, different, and exciting. Editors and reporters see thousands of dull, sitting-at-the-desk photos every year. Come up with a creative way to showcase something photogenic about your business . . . and make it stand out from the pack.

7. *Follow up.* Following up is the key to securing coverage. Wait four to six days after you've sent the information, then follow up your pitch letter, and/or press release, with an email or telephone call. If you don't hear from them in a week, follow up. If they request additional information, send it immediately—do not wait until the next day—and follow up to confirm receipt.

TIP

One of the best ways to get free publicity for your product is having it in the hands of buyers. For example, when one prominent scooter manufacturer wanted to bring back the popularity of scooters for kids, they decided the best way to market it was to give out scooters and helmets to kids in a specific age range (with their parents' permission) to ride in various parks. Needless to say, when a few kids were seen riding these new scooters, every kid in the neighborhood wanted one.

Talking to the Media

Once you reach the editor, reporter, journalist, blogger, etc., remember they are extremely busy and probably on deadline. Be courteous, and ask if they have time to talk. If not, offer to call back at a more convenient time. If they can talk to you, keep your initial pitch to 20 seconds in which you elaborate a little on what you already sent. This way, you're not repeating yourself, only extending the storyline slightly. (Hint: Have this brief conversation prepared and rehearsed, so you don't get nervous. Then offer to send written information, and/or photos if it's a visual medium, to support your story ideas.

The following tips will boost your chances of success:

- *If your idea gets rejected, ask if they can recommend someone else who might be interested.*

- *Know exactly what you're going to say before you call the reporter.* Have it written down in front of you—it's easier, and you'll feel more confident. But be prepared for questions as well.
- *Be persistent.* Remember, not everyone will be interested. If your story idea is turned down, try to find out why and use that information to improve your next pitch. Just keep going and don't give up. You will succeed eventually.
- *Don't be a pest.* You can easily be persistent without being annoying.
- *Be helpful and become a resource by providing information.* Remember, story editors need stories and websites need content. There are only so many they can come up with on their own.

Meet the Press

Think of a press release as your ticket to publicity. Editors, journalists, producers, and reporters get hundreds of press releases a week. How do you make yours stand out?

First, be sure you have a good reason for sending a press release. A grand opening, a new product, a new location, an impressive award, a special event, or perhaps a celebrity spokesperson are all good reasons.

Second, make sure your press release is appropriately targeted for the website, publication, or broadcast media you're sending it to. The editor of *Road & Track*, for example, is not going to be interested in the new organic baby pacifier you've invented. It sounds obvious, but many entrepreneurs make the mistake of sending press releases at random without considering the target audience.

Most press releases today are sent via email, double-spaced with an eye-catching headline and a dateline such as New York City, January 4, 2021. Limit your press release to one or two pages at most. It should be just long enough to cover the six basic elements: who, what, when, where, why, and how. It should also focus on the value you are providing to the audience.

Provide answers to the questions: Why will their target audience, which should be similar to your own, want to read or hear this story? What can they gain from reading it? Remember, if it's of interest to them, it can translate into business for you. If it's only of interest to you (or self-indulgent), it's a waste of your time.

Don't embellish or hype the information. Remember, you are not writing the article; you are merely presenting the information and showing why it is relevant in hopes that they will write about it. Pay close attention to grammar and spelling. Competition for publicity is intense, and a press release full of typos or errors is more likely to get tossed aside.

Some business owners use attention-getting gimmicks to get their press releases noticed. In most cases, this is a waste of money. If your release is well-written and relevant, you don't need to send along a silly gift item or a bouquet of flowers to get your message across (and most recipients will roll their eyes at such nonsense).

TIP

Never tell a reporter they should cover your story because you advertise with their publication. Avoid mentioning advertising relationships with their outlet, or they may feel you expect a level of quid pro quo and will be less likely to "bite" at your story, even if they think it's worthwhile.

- *Always remember that assistants get promoted.* Be nice to everyone you speak with, no matter how low they are on the totem pole. After you establish a connection, keep in touch; people get promoted, and it's nice to have a rapport with them. If someone leaves a company, try to get to know their replacement and try to find out where the person who left is now working—it might give you a lead to another publication or website.

- *Say thank you.* When you succeed in getting publicity for your business, always send an email or even a note saying thank you to the story editor, producer, or reporter who worked on it with you. You'd be surprised how much a note means.

Plan your publicity efforts as carefully as the rest of your business. You'll be glad you made the effort when you see your company featured in the news—and the results in your bottom line.

Special Events

Ever since the first Wild West Show was staged to sell "Doctor Winthrop's Miracle Elixir," businesspeople have understood the value of promotional events.

Special events (such as contests, street fairs, local concerts, seminars, and webinars) are one of the fastest-growing areas of marketing today. And while large corporations shell out billions each year to host events, small companies, too, can use promotions to reach their market in a way no conventional method can.

No matter how spectacular an event is, however, it can't stand alone. You can use advertising or public relations without doing a special event, but you need both advertising and public relations to make your event work. How do you put together the right mix to make your event successful?

First, you must know what you want to accomplish. The desired outcome of event marketing is no different from that of any other marketing effort: You want to draw attention to your product or service, create greater awareness of it, and increase sales.

While there are numerous opportunities, here are a few long-time favorites.

Grand Openings

You're excited about opening your new business. Everyone else will be, too . . . right? Wrong. You have to create the excitement, and a knockout grand opening celebration is the way to do it. From start to finish, your event has to scream "We're here. We're open. We're ready to go. We're better than, different from, and more eager to serve you than our competitors. We want to get to know you and have you do business with us."

A grand opening is one of the best reasons to stage a special event. No one thinks twice about why you're blowing your own horn. They show up to have fun, and when they think about your event, they'll remember what a great time they had. Then they'll be back to check out your business. In an age of Covid-19, you may need to hold outdoor events, and spread them out over a full day to limit the number of people who can attend at any given time. Have hand sanitizer near any items that guests can touch and spread out lines for food, or anything else, so that people stand six feet apart. And everyone attending should wear masks. If a virtual event will work, go for it, as long as it's fun for everyone involved. Remember to ask people to please stay on mute until asked to speak. While you can't give away food virtually, you can do all kinds of fun video presentations, offer discount coupons, and set up links from which attendees can win prizes.

Social Graces

Does your business use recycled paper products or donate to a homeless shelter? Today, many consumers consider such factors when deciding whether to patronize your business. The "social responsibility" quotient of your business is important today, so join in and make a difference. Besides doing something good, it can also help your bottom line.

If you think getting involved in social causes would work for your business, here are some things to consider. First and foremost, customers can smell "phony" social responsibility a mile away, so unless you're really committed to a cause, don't try to exploit customers' concerns to make a profit.

Consider these steps for making social responsibility work for you and your community:

- *Set goals.* What do you want to achieve? What do you want your company to achieve? Do you want to enter a new market? Introduce a new product? Enhance the image of your business?
- *Decide what cause you want to align yourself with.* This may be your toughest decision, considering all the options out there: children, the environment, senior citizens, homeless people, people with disabilities—the list goes on. Consider a cause that fits with your products or services; for example, a manufacturer of women's clothing could get involved in funding breast cancer research. Another way to narrow the field is by considering not only causes you feel strongly about, but also those with which your customers are aligned.
- *Choose a nonprofit or other organization to partner with.* Get to know the group, and make sure it's sound, upstanding, geographically convenient, and willing to cooperate with you in developing a partnership.
- *Design a program, and propose it to the nonprofit group.* Besides laying out what you plan to accomplish, also include indicators that will measure the program's success in tangible terms.
- *Negotiate an agreement with the organization.* Know what they want before you sit down, and try to address their concerns upfront.
- *Involve employees.* Unless you get employees involved from the beginning, they won't be able to communicate the real caring involved in the campaign to customers.
- *Involve customers.* Don't just do something good and tell your customers about it later. Get customers involved, too. Have a way they can donate money or help with something like a walk-a-thon.

It's to your advantage not to have a run-of-the-mill, garden-variety ribbon-cutting. Be original. Come up with a theme that fits

your business. Design a terrific invitation, do plenty of publiciz-
ing, provide good food and great entertainment, select a give-
away that promotes your business (and draws people to your
store, restaurant, studio, office, warehouse, or onto your website),
and incorporate some way of tracking who attended your event
(sign-in/guest list, contest entry forms, raffle, coupons, birthday
club sign-ups, and so on). Again, this can be done virtually.

AHA!

Whenever possible, tie your business to a current event or trend. Does
your product or service somehow relate to the Olympics, the presiden-
tial election, the environment, or the hot PlayStation games? Whether
you're planning a special event or just sending out a press release,
you can gain publicity by association. Hint: Make sure it's a realistic
connection. Don't try to tie your business in with something that has
no real relevance.

Entertainment and Attractions

Time, space, popular appeal, and suitability are four things to
consider when you host or sponsor a one-time special attraction.
If space permits and a beach motif fits your business, having a
huge sandcastle built in your parking lot might draw attention
and business for the entire time it takes to construct it.

Just keep in mind that the novelties and entertainment
shouldn't last so long or be so distracting that no one finds the
time or inclination to do business with you. You also don't want
to distract your business neighbors. Think of these events as the
appetizer with your product or service as the main course.

What Is Social Entrepreneurship?

What, exactly, is social entrepreneurship? It isn't always clear. Some people view adding a social mission as a way to help others or give back (for example, giving 3 percent of profits to a charity you care about); others see it as a core of their strategy (for instance, Toms Shoes gives a pair of shoes to a child in need for every pair it sells); and others do it as an add-on (e.g., consultancies or software firms that do pro bono work as a percentage of hours billed).

True social entrepreneurs see themselves as agents of change. They see their business (or the profits from it) as a way to tackle a social problem. Broadly defined, it is the mechanism by which the private sector helps solve public and private sector problems that are not being addressed. Traditional entrepreneurs look for opportunities in new markets, need to return capital to investors, and require scale. So do social entrepreneurs, albeit sometimes differently.

The key distinguisher is the "why" of starting a business. An entrepreneur is in business to deliver a bottom-line profit for serving a market in a better or more efficient manner. Social entrepreneurs have a triple bottom line that they consider: people, planet, and profit. They're typically not looking to solve an immediate problem. Instead, they're looking for scalable, wholesale change to the underlying condition that led to the problem.

Social entrepreneurs want to make money so they can make a difference in something they are deeply passionate about—and the social good element is core to their mission and strategy.

Holidays and Seasons

Some of the most common and easily developed special events are based on holidays or times of year.

Again, when planning an event tied to a holiday or season, make originality your motto. If the average December temperature in your city is a balmy 76 degrees, don't dredge up icicles and fake snow for the store. Take a cue from your locale: Put antlers on pink flamingos and dress Santa in shorts and sunglasses.

Celebrity Appearances

Working with celebrities is like buying a volatile stock—high risk but high return. If you are willing to go out on a limb, you may harvest the sweetest fruit. Many celebrities are affable, cooperative, and generous if they are treated professionally and supplied with all the necessary details in advance.

The key to using a celebrity to promote your business is knowing what kind of "personality" is appropriate for your company and marketing goals. Think about whom you want to attract, what kind of media coverage you want to generate, and what kind of impression you want to create.

Whether you are seeking soap stars, sports stars, or movie stars, it's usually best to contact their agents first. If you don't know who a star's agent is, do a search online. Major celebrities often have booking agents and even commercial agents; try a few choices and you're likely to get the information you need. Then call and ask who represents that individual so you can send an email regarding whomever it is you are seeking. It's not hard to find out who represents someone—it's hard to get them to agree to show up or work with you. If you are teaming up for a good cause, that might help your case. Remember, however, that major, and even minor, celebrities have busy schedules. Considering Covid-19, you may opt for virtual celebrity appearances.

Unless you know celebrities personally, you must consider the arrangement a commercial venture for them. There are literally hundreds of details to work out and opportunities at every turn for something to go wrong unless you are experienced in dealing with celebrities or you have contacted a reputable talent or public relations agency to help you.

Celebrities don't have to be nationally known names, either. Think about local celebrities in your community who might be willing to be part of your special event. A politician, well-known businessperson, community leader, or even a popular athlete now playing at the collegiate level can be an excellent addition to your big day.

You're the Expert

As an entrepreneur, it's your responsibility to get your business noticed—which means you've got to toot your own horn. You need to do whatever it takes to let others know you exist and that you are an expert source of information or advice about your industry. But first you need to study your industry, read as much as you can, and gain the expertise that people will expect from you.

Being regarded as an industry expert can do wonders for your business. How can you get your expertise known?

- Start by making sure you know everything you can about your business, product, and industry.
- Contact experts in the field, and ask them how they became experts.
- Talk to as many groups as possible. (If public speaking strikes fear in your heart, you'd better get over it. This is one skill you're going to need as an entrepreneur. Try a Toastmasters group or practice among friends to boost your confidence and skills.) Volunteer to talk to key organizations, service clubs, business groups, a Rotary Club, or chamber of commerce . . . whoever might be interested in what you have to say. Do it free of charge, of course, and keep it fun, interesting, and timely.
- Contact industry trade publications and volunteer to write articles, opinion pieces, blogs, or columns for websites, as well as print media. (If you can't do that, write a letter to the editor.)
- Offer seminars or demonstrations related to your business (a caterer could explain how to cook Thai food, for instance).
- Host (or be a guest on) a local radio or TV talk show. Email local producers.

Hint: Make your presentation, article, guest radio appearance, or whatever you decide to do about the topic, not about you or even your business. You will be introduced as the owner of your business and an expert in your industry, and you can talk about some of your experiences. But if the article, blog, or interview sounds like a lengthy advertisement, people will get restless. Self-promotion often needs to be subtle, and in this case, it's your expertise and even anecdotes that will bring them to your business, not an endless sales pitch.

Co-Sponsoring

You can partner with complementary businesses to host an event, or you can take part as a sponsor of an established charity or public cause. Sporting events, fairs, and festivals have proved to be popular choices with good track records for achieving marketing goals. Keep in mind, not every event is right for every business. As with any marketing strategy, your event must be suited to your customers' needs.

Think about how your company can benefit any event. If you are a florist, for instance, you could provide flowers for a wide range of charity luncheons or galas. A health-food retailer could provide free energy bars to participants in a local 10K race. Whatever you do, be sure to promote it with press releases, a sign in your window, and/or a mention in the event's program.

Anniversary Celebrations

This is one special event most people can relate to. Staying in business for several years is something to be proud of, so why not share the achievement with others? It offers you a great opportunity to throw a party and invite current, past, and prospective customers to enjoy your anniversary, too. Once again, you may need to consider Covid-19 protocol such as masks and distancing between people.

Games, Contests, and Raffles

From naming a mascot to guessing the number of jelly beans in a jar, contests have long been proven to be a great means of attracting attention. But they pay off big only when they're properly promoted and ethically managed. Be sure your prizes are first-rate and that you get the word out in a timely and professional manner. Let people know how and when they can participate. Think through all the ramifications of judging and selecting and awarding a prize. Check out the need for special permits or licenses well before staging any contest or raffle (it never hurts to get a legal opinion just to be on the safe side). Above all, deliver on your promises. Again, partnering with a good cause can bring in more people.

WARNING

Before sponsoring a contest or giving away a prize, make sure you contact the Federal Trade Commission (FTC), a lawyer specializing in games and promotions, or your secretary of state's office to check out the FTC guidelines governing different types of promotions in your city or state.

Networking

The ability to network is one of the most crucial skills any startup entrepreneur can have. How else will you meet the clients and contacts necessary to grow your business?

But many people are put off by the idea of networking, thinking it requires a phony, glad-handing personality that oozes insincerity. Nothing could be further from the truth. Today, you have the power to network with millions of people. Social media may have taken the lead in networking opportunities. However, there are so many other ways you can network, from attending conferences or seminars to joining organizations.

Think a moment. What do good networkers do? How do they act? What is their basic attitude? You'll probably be surprised at how much you instinctively know about the subject.

You may decide, for example, that a good networker should be outgoing, sincere, friendly, supportive, a good listener, or someone who follows up and stays in touch. To determine other skills an effective networker needs, simply ask yourself "How do I like to be treated? What kinds of people do I trust and consider good friends?"

Now that you have an idea of what attributes a good networker must have, take an objective look at your own interactive abilities. Do you consider yourself shy and regard networking groups as threatening? Do you tend to do all the talking in a conversation? Do you give other people referrals and ideas without a thought to your own personal gain? Can people count on you keeping your word?

Many people go to networking events, but very few know how to network effectively. Networking is more than just getting out and meeting people. Networking is a structured plan to get to know people who will do business with you or introduce you to those who will. It is not a place to be the in-your-face salesperson. We've all met people like that at parties who are constantly trying to sell you something. They're annoying—don't be one of those people.

The best way to succeed at networking is to make a plan, commit to it, learn networking skills, and execute your plan. To make the best plan, ask yourself: What do I want to achieve? How many leads (prospects) do I want per month? Where do my customers and prospects go to network? What business organizations would benefit my business? How can I build my image and the image of my business? What would I like to volunteer to do in the community?

Know Your Networks

First, it's important to mention that you don't need to go to networking groups to network successfully. You can meet people who may be significant contacts anywhere.

There are, however, four main types of networking groups. What will work best for you depends on your goals and needs.

1. *Casual contact networks.* These are general business groups that allow many people from various professions. These groups usually meet monthly and some hold mixers where everyone mingles informally. The best examples are chambers of commerce. You can make initial contacts that will be valuable in other aspects of developing your referral business. But because casual-contact organizations aren't tailored primarily to help you get referrals, you have to exert effort to make them work.

2. *Strong contact networks.* Organizations whose purpose is principally to help members exchange business referrals are known as strong contact referral groups. Some of these groups meet weekly, typically over lunch or breakfast. Most of them limit membership to one member per profession or specialty. Strong contact networks provide highly focused opportunities for you and your associates to begin developing your referral marketing campaigns. But be prepared to devote time to attend meetings regularly and to help fellow group members.

3. *Community service clubs.* Unlike more business-oriented groups, service groups aren't set up primarily for referral networking; their activities are focused on service to the community. However, while giving time and effort to civic causes, you form lasting relationships that broaden and deepen your personal and business networks. If you go in not to benefit but to contribute, the social capital you accrue will eventually reward you in other ways and from other directions—business among them.

4. *Professional associations.* Professional association members tend to be from one specific type of industry, such as banking, architecture, personnel, accounting, or health. The primary purpose of a professional association is to exchange information and ideas. Your goal in tapping into such networks is to join groups that contain your potential clients or target markets. Ask your best clients or customers which groups they belong to so you can find the right one for you.

Try out a networking group before joining—most will have some event(s) open to prospective members. Some groups have a variety of outgoing people happy to talk to newcomers and listen as well. Others suffer from a clique mentality or are overrun with realtors and insurance salespeople trying to sell, sell, sell. See if you like the people. Are they friendly or standoffish? Do they listen to you or only talk about themselves? Do they network, or is the group just an excuse for a social meeting where gossip and personal conversations prevail? Do some scouting and see if there's a networking group for you. Network groups run the gamut—some people swear by their group, others swear at their networking group. Also, remember, networking is a two-way street—it's about giving *and* receiving.

Today, many networking groups meet virtually, some because of Covid-19 protocol, others because of logistics with members working from locations in various parts of the country or the world. This makes it easier to attend meetings, although some people are uncomfortable speaking up in virtual events. If that's the case, you may sit and listen at first. You'll usually find that whoever is hosting the networking event will ask you to say a little about yourself—that's when it's time to unmute and introduce yourself and your business—if you want, you can prepare something in advance, but practice first so it does not sound like you are reading.

Make a networking plan listing your five best customers, five targeted prime prospects, and five targeted organizations. Next, set goals for involvement in each organization, determine how much time you will need to commit to each organization and prospect, and decide what kinds of results you expect. And finally, open your horizons.

Now that you have a plan, get committed. Tell yourself that you will devote enough time and effort to make it work. Half the battle of networking is getting out there and in the swim.

The other half of the battle is learning to network effectively. Typically, ineffective networkers attend several networking groups but visit with the same friends each time. Avoid that at all costs. Ineffective networkers also tend to get involved and expect only to receive invitations and information rather than participate and bring something to the table, too. Obviously, this behavior defeats the entire purpose of networking. If you stick with familiar faces, you never meet anyone new. And because most people stay within their circle of friends, newcomers view the organization as a group of cliques. This is one reason people fear going to new organizations by themselves—they're afraid no one will notice them.

TIP

After you finish talking to someone at a networking event, take a few seconds to jot down pertinent information on the back of their business card. This can be anything from their company's biggest problem to the college their daughter attends—whatever will give you a "hook" to follow up on when you call them later. And look for their profile on LinkedIn. Ask to connect with a personal message reminding them of how you met; consider including a link to an article that is related to their business or a challenge they mentioned.

The trick with networking is to be proactive. This means taking control of the situation instead of just reacting to it. Networking requires going beyond your comfort zone and challenging yourself. Try these tips:

- *Set a goal to meet five or more new people at each event.* Whenever you attend a group, whether a party, an industry luncheon, or a mixer, make a point of heading straight for people you don't know. Greet the newcomers (they will love you for it!). If you don't make this goal a habit, you'll naturally gravitate toward the same old acquaintances.
- *Try one or two new groups per month.* You can attend almost any organization's meetings a few times before you must join. This is another way to stretch yourself and make a new set of contacts. Determine what business organizations and activities you would best fit into. It may be the chamber of commerce, the arts council, a museum society, a civic organization, a baseball league, a computer club, or the PTA. Attend every function you can that synergizes your goals and customer/prospect interaction.
- *Carry your business cards with you everywhere.* After all, you never know when you might meet a key contact, and if you don't have your cards with you, you lose out. Take your cards to church, the gym, parties, the grocery store—even while walking the dog.
- *Don't make a beeline for your seat.* Frequently, you'll see people at networking groups sitting at the dinner table staring into space—half an hour before the meal is due to start. Why are they sitting alone? Take full advantage of the valuable networking time before you have to sit down. Once the meeting starts, you won't be able to mingle.

AHA!

Always be alert to networking opportunities. Don't rule out traffic school, Little League games, aerobics class, other nonbusiness events, or even weekend brunch or your church coffee hour as chances to share your story. Leisure activities provide a natural setting for networking and encourage relationship-building. These are great places to meet people, but don't start talking business at nonbusiness events, and remember you do not want to become that always annoying salesperson whom people can't wait to get away from. The same goes for social media—get to know people first. If they ask what you do—and they will—make the first encounters ones in which you simply "tell them, don't sell them."

- *Don't sit by people you know.* Mealtime is a prime time for meeting new people. You may be in that seat for several hours, so don't limit your opportunities by sitting with your friends. This is a wonderful chance to get to know new people on either side of you. Remember, you are spending precious time and money to attend this event. Get your money's worth; you can talk to your friends some other time. Make a point of circulating, or as they say, "work the room."
- *Listen more than you talk.* Yes, you want to tell them all about yourself, but you can do that gradually. Listen to what they say—ask a couple of questions so they can see you are listening and interested. When you do talk, tell interesting, concise stories. Think short, memorable sound bites.
- *Don't just hand them a business card—make it more important.* Say something like "Let me give you my card," and as you hand it to them, add "I look forward to speaking with you and the prospect of working together." If you feel good about your interactions, you could say "If next week works, I'll give you a call." Also ask for their card.
- *Smile and be approachable.* If you want people to talk to you, be

approachable. If you're standing with your arms folded or staring at your cell phone, they will not come over to you. In fact, shut the phone off and put it in your pocket or your purse. When people do approach you, smile—show them that you are genuinely glad to meet them. Starting off with small talk is fine, but avoid complaining or making a potentially bad joke. Humor can be hit or miss when you don't know someone. And finally, if you are talking to a group of people, include everyone. Don't have a one-on-one conversation leaving five other people standing there—it's rude.

Image Power

Throughout this book, we've touched on various aspects of developing a corporate image. Your business cards, logo, website, social media pages, signage, and letterhead all tie into that image. So do your marketing materials and ads. It's equally important to keep your image in mind when planning a publicity campaign.

The websites, social media platforms, publications, and broadcast stations you target with your publicity must also fit your image. A company that makes clothes targeted at teenage skateboarders would prefer publicity on a website geared for "boarders" or in a cutting-edge lifestyle magazine rather than in a mainstream publication aimed at business executives. Think about how the website, publication, or broadcast will affect your image, and make sure the results will be positive.

Don't forget the most important parts of your public image: yourself and your employees. Your marketing materials and corporate sponsorships can tout your socially responsible, kindhearted company, but if your employees are rude and uncaring toward customers, all your efforts to promote that image will be in vain.

Make sure your employees understand the image you are trying to convey to customers and how they contribute to maintaining that image. Lead by example and show them how you want them to behave whenever they're in the public eye.

- *Be friendly and helpful.* Make people feel welcome. Find out what brought them there, and see if there's any way you can help them. Introduce them to others, make business suggestions, or give them a referral. Not only will you probably make a friend, but putting others at ease eliminates self-consciousness. A side benefit: If you make the effort to help others, you'll soon find people helping you.

- *Set a goal for what you expect from each meeting.* Your goals can vary from meeting to meeting. Some examples might be learning from the speaker's topic, discovering industry trends, looking for new prospects, or connecting with peers. If you work out of your home, you may find your purpose is simply to get out and talk to people face to face. Focusing your mind on your goal before you even walk into the event keeps you on target.

- *Be willing to give to receive.* We said it before, but it's worth saying again: Networking is a two-way street. Don't expect new contacts to shower you with referrals and business unless you are equally generous. Follow up with your contacts; keep in touch; always share information or leads that might benefit them. You'll be paid back tenfold for your thoughtfulness.

The Meet Market

To make the most of any networking situation, make sure to heed the following dos and don'ts:

- *Don't spend too much time with one person,* or you defeat the purpose of networking. Your objective is to take advantage of the entire room. If you spend three minutes with a prospect, that gives you a possibility of 20 contacts per hour. Spending five minutes with each person reduces that to 12 contacts and so on.

- *Do know the kinds of problems you can solve* rather than a bunch of boring facts about your product or service. Talk in terms of how you benefit customers rather than the product or service you offer.

- *Don't be negative.* Never complain about or bad-mouth a person or business. You never know whether the prospect you're talking to has some connection, interest, relationship, or affiliation with the people, company, or product you're slamming.
- *Don't forget your manners.* "Please" and "thank you" go a long way toward creating a good impression.
- *Do be prepared.* When people ask you what you do, be ready to describe your business in one short, interesting sentence that intrigues and enlightens; follow up with something appropriately personal and ask the same of the other people present.

CHAPTER 7
Sell It!

Effective Selling Techniques

NO MATTER WHAT BUSINESS YOU'RE IN, if you're an entrepreneur, you're in sales. "But I hate to sell," you groan. You're not alone. Many people are intimidated by selling—either because they're not sure how to proceed or they think they don't have the "right" personality to sell.

Well, guess what? Anyone can sell—anyone, that is, who can learn to connect with the customer, listen to their needs, and offer the right solutions. In fact, as the founder of your business, you're better positioned than anyone to sell your products and services. Even if you have a team of crack salespeople, there's no one else who has the same passion for, understanding of, and enthusiasm about your products or services as you. And once you finish reading this chapter, you'll have plenty of sales skills as well.

Understanding Your Unique Selling Proposition

Before you can begin selling your products or services to anyone else, you have to sell yourself on them. This is especially important because your products or services are usually similar to those around you. Very few businesses are one of a kind. Just look around you: How many clothing retailers, hardware stores, nail salons, health-food stores, and electricians are truly unique?

The key to effective selling in this situation is what advertising and marketing professionals call a unique selling proposition (USP). Unless you can pinpoint what makes your business unique in a world of homogeneous competitors, you cannot target your sales efforts successfully.

Pinpointing your USP requires some hard soul-searching and creativity. One way to start is to analyze how other companies use their USPs to their advantage. This requires careful analysis of other companies' ads and marketing messages. If you analyze what they say they sell, not just the characteristics of their products or services, you can learn a great deal about how companies distinguish themselves from competitors.

For example, Joseph Revson, founder of Revlon, always used to say he sold hope, not makeup. Some airlines sell friendly service, while others sell on-time service. Neiman Marcus sells luxury, Walmart sells bargains, and Disney sells dreams and fantasies.

AHA!

Want to boost sales? Offer a 100 percent guarantee. This minimizes customer objections and shows you believe in your product or service. Product guarantees should be unconditional, with no hidden clauses like "guaranteed for 30 days." Use guarantees for services, too: "Satisfaction guaranteed. You'll be thrilled with our service, or we'll redo it at our expense." This will also motivate you and your employees to always give your best.

Star Power

You can find salespeople with a wide range of temperaments and styles of selling. Some are more aggressive than others. Some are more consultative. Some are highly educated, some not so much. But they're all champions because they're the ones who consistently build the business, keep the territory, and retain their customers. And they share these three traits:

1. *Attitude.* Attitude makes all the difference. Sales champions set priorities and keep things moving forward, ending each day with a sense of accomplishment. Sales champions don't let losing a deal get them down. If they can't change a situation, they change their attitude about it. In sales, you've got to make things happen for your business—and the best salespeople can't wait to get started every day.

2. *Tenacity.* When sales champions know they have something of value for a prospect or client, they don't give up. They learn more about the situation, the potential customer, and the customer's company. If they can't make a sale on the first attempt, they study what went wrong and improve their approach for the next time so they can come back with new ideas. They are not easily defeated. However, sales champions understand when they're wasting time and when it's best to move on to the next tactic or even the next sale. If you get smarter each time you come back, you will succeed. When prospects see how much you believe in your vision and in helping them reach their goals, they, too, will be enthusiastic about what you have to offer.

3. *Follow-through.* A broken promise makes it extremely difficult to regain a customer's trust. Sales champions don't make promises they can't keep. They don't try to be everything to everybody. But once they give their word, they stick to it.

A sales champion doesn't exhibit all these traits all the time. But they know that in the end, the harder they work at sharpening these traits, the better these traits will work for them.

Each of these is an example of a company that has found a USP "peg" on which to hang its marketing strategy. A business can peg its USP on product characteristics, price structure, placement strategy (location and distribution), or promotional strategy. These are what marketers call the "four P's" of marketing. They are manipulated to give a business a market position that sets it apart from the competition.

Sometimes a company focuses on one particular "peg," which also drives the strategy in other areas. A classic example is Hanes L'eggs hosiery. Back in an era when hosiery was sold primarily in department stores, Hanes opened a new distribution channel for hosiery sales. The idea: Because hosiery was a consumer staple, why not sell it where other staples were sold—in grocery stores?

That placement strategy also drove the company's selection of product packaging (a plastic egg), so the pantyhose did not seem incongruent in a supermarket. And because the product did not have to be pressed and wrapped in tissue and boxes, it could be priced lower than other brands.

Here's how to uncover your USP and use it to power up your sales:

- *Put yourself in your customer's shoes.* Too often, entrepreneurs fall in love with their product or service and forget that it is the customer's needs, not their own, that they must satisfy. Step back from your daily operations and scrutinize what your customers really want. Suppose you own a pizza parlor. Sure, customers come into your pizza place for food. But is food all they want? What could make them come back again and again and ignore your competition? The answer might be quality, convenience, reliability, friendliness, cleanliness, courtesy, or customer service. Or it could be that you've got enough seating that they can chat with friends—thus you provide a gathering place. It might be as simple as the fact that you remember their name and ask about their children when they pick up an order.

  Remember, price is never the only reason people buy. If your competition is beating you on pricing because they are larger, you have to find another sales feature that addresses the customer's needs and then build your sales and promotional efforts around that feature.

- *Know what motivates your customers' behavior and buying decisions.* Effective marketing requires you to be an amateur psychologist. You need to know what drives and motivates customers. Go beyond the traditional customer demographics, such as age, gender, race, income, and geographic location, that most businesses collect to analyze their sales trends. For our pizza shop example, it is not enough to know that 75 percent of your customers are in the 18-to-25-age range. You need to look at their motives for buying pizza—taste, peer pressure, convenience, and so on.

  Cosmetics companies are great examples of industries that know the value of psychologically oriented promotion. People buy these products based on their desires (for a prettier face, luxury, glamour, and so on), not on their needs.

WARNING
Want to know the best way to talk yourself out of a sale? Overselling—pushing your features and benefits too hard—is a common problem for salespeople. The problem is that you aren't hearing the customer's needs. Shut up and listen. Then start asking questions. Keep asking questions until you can explain how your product or service meets the customer's needs.

- *Uncover the real reasons customers buy your product instead of a competitor's.* As your business grows, you'll be able to ask your best source of information: your customers. For example, the pizza entrepreneur could ask them why they like his pizza over others, plus ask them to rate the importance of the features he offers, such as taste, size, ingredients, atmosphere, and service. You can also use surveys to get new ideas from your customers. You will be surprised how honest people are when you ask how you can improve your service.

Because your business is just starting out, you won't have a lot of customers to ask yet, so "shop" your competition instead. Many retailers routinely drop into their competitors' stores to see what and how they are selling. If you are brave, try asking a few of the customers after they leave the premises what they like and dislike about the competitor's products and services.

Once you have gone through this three-step market intelligence process, you need to take the next—and hardest—step, clearing your mind of any preconceived ideas about your products or services and being brutally honest. What features of your business jump out at you as something that sets you apart? What can you promote that will make customers want to patronize your business? How can you position your business to highlight your USP?

Do not get discouraged. Successful business ownership is not about having unique products or services; it's about making your products or services stand out—even in a market filled with similar items.

TIP

Tips for better calls: Stand up when you talk on the phone. It puts power and confidence in your voice. Smile when you say hello. It makes you sound relaxed and confident. Prospects can't see these telephone tricks, but they'll hear and feel the difference in your tone—and in your persuasive powers.

Making Sales Presentations

Once you have reeled in a prospect through networking, social media, emails, webinars, or simply from a recommendation from a friend, vendor, customer, or co-worker you need to have a plan for success. Four elements determine whether a sale will be made or not:

1. *Rapport*: putting yourself on the same side of the fence as the prospect
2. *Need*: determining what factors will motivate the prospect to listen with the intent to purchase
3. *Importance*: the weight the prospect assigns to a product, feature, benefit, price, or time frame
4. *Confidence*: your ability to project credibility, to remove doubt, and to gain the prospect's belief that the risk of purchase will be less than the reward of ownership

Here is a closer look at the steps you can take to make your sales presentation a success.

Before the Presentation

- *Know your customer's business.* Potential clients expect you to know their business, customers, and competition as well as you know your own product or service. Study your customer's industry. Know its problems and trends. Find out who the company's biggest competitors are. Some research tools include the company's website, annual report, brochures, catalogs, and newsletters. You can also do an online search, and look at trade publications and/or chamber of commerce directories.
- *Write out your sales presentation.* Making a sales presentation isn't something you do on the fly. Always use a written presentation. The basic structure of any sales presentation includes five key points: Build rapport with your prospect, introduce the business topic, ask questions to better under-

stand your prospect's needs, summarize your key selling points, and close the sale. Think about the three major selling points of your products or services. Develop leading questions to probe your customer's reactions and needs.

- *Make sure you are talking to the right person.* This seems elementary, but many salespeople neglect to do it. Then at the last minute, the buyer wriggles off the hook by saying they need a boss's, spouse's, or partner's approval. When you are setting the appointment, always ask "Are you the one I should be talking to, or are there others who will be making the buying decision?"

AHA!

Condition prospects to say yes by asking questions they will agree with, such as "It's a great day, isn't it?" or "You got an early start today, didn't you?" Little questions like these will help start customers on a momentum that builds trust. Subconsciously, because they are agreeing with you, they begin to trust you.

In the Customer's Office Or on a Zoom Call

- *Build rapport.* Before you start discussing business, build rapport with your prospect. To accomplish this, do some homework. Find out if you have a colleague in common. Has the prospect's company been in the news lately? Are they interested in sports? Get a little insight into the company and the individual so you can make the rapport genuine.
- *Ask questions.* Don't jump into a canned sales spiel. The most effective way to sell is to ask the prospect questions and see where they lead you. (Of course, your questions are carefully structured to elicit the prospect's needs—ones that your products or services just happen to be able to fill.)

Ask questions that require more than a yes or no

response, and that deal with more than just costs, price, procedures, and the technical aspects of the prospect's business. Most important, ask questions that will reveal the prospect's motivation to purchase, their problems and needs, and the prospect's decision-making processes. Don't be afraid to ask a client why they feel a certain way. That's how you'll get to understand your customers.

- *Take notes.* Don't rely on your memory to remind you of what's important to your prospect. Ask upfront if it's all right for you to take notes during your sales presentation. Write down key points you can refer to later during your presentation.

- *Be sure to write down objections.* This shows your prospect you are truly listening. In this way, you can specifically answer objections by showing how the customer will benefit from your product or service. It could be, for instance, by saving money, raising productivity, increasing employee motivation, or increasing their company's name recognition.

- *Learn to listen.* Salespeople who do all the talking during a presentation not only bore the prospect, but also generally lose the sale. A good rule of thumb is to listen 70 percent of the time and talk 30 percent of the time. Don't interrupt. It's tempting to step in and tell the prospect something you think is vitally important. Before you speak, ask yourself if what you're about to say is really necessary.

When you do speak, focus on asking questions. Pretend you're Katie Couric interviewing a movie star: Ask questions, then shut up. You can improve your listening skills by taking notes and observing your prospect's body language, not jumping to conclusions.

Presentation Perfect

Want to improve your sales presentation skills? Use these strategies to hone your speaking abilities:

- *Tag-team-sell for evaluation purposes.* Have a colleague go on sales calls or zoom calls with you once a week to listen to your presentation. Create a review form for them to fill out immediately after your performance. Include your strengths as well as your weaknesses. Read it right away, and talk about what you can do to improve.

- *Record your telephone and online sales conversations.* Use them as a self-monitor of your ability to present a clear and confident message. Play them back. If you can't stand your voice, change your pitch. Or ask a trusted friend or mentor to listen to your tone and give feedback—sometimes we are really our own worst critics, and many people cringe at the sound of their own voice for no real reason.

- *Read a chapter from a sales book aloud, and make an audio recording of it.* Play it in your car. You'll learn about sales and about how you present your pitch. Would you buy from yourself? If not, record another version with style and emotion.

- *Record video of the first five minutes of your sales presentation.* Ask a friend or colleague to be the prospect. Watch the video together, and rate your performance. Repeat the process once a week for two months. Work to eliminate your two worst habits; at the same time, work to enhance your two best strengths.

- *Above all, be yourself.* Don't put on an act. Your personality will shine if you believe in what you are saying. Being genuine will win the prospect's confidence . . . and the sale.

AHA!

Offer a first-time incentive to help clinch the sale. If prospects like your product or service, they'll be inclined to make a decision now rather than wait a few days or put off the decision indefinitely. First-time incentives might include "10 percent off with your purchase today" or "With today's purchase, you'll receive one free hour of consultation."

- *Answer objections with "feel," "felt," and "found."* Don't argue when a prospect says "I'm not interested," "I just bought one," or "I don't have time right now." Simply say "I understand how you feel. A lot of my present customers felt the same way. But when they found out how much time they saved by using our product, they were amazed." Then ask for an appointment. Prospects like to hear about other people who have been in a similar situation.
- *Probe deeper.* If a prospect tells you "We're looking for cost savings and efficiency," will you immediately tell them how your product meets their need for cost savings and efficiency? A really smart salesperson won't—they will ask more questions and probe deeper: "I understand why that is important. Can you give me a specific example?" Asking for more information—and listening to the answers— enables you to better position your product and show you understand the client's needs.
- *Find the "hot button."* A customer may have a long list of needs, but there is usually one "hot button" that will get the person to buy. This is also commonly referred to as a "pain point." The key to the hot button or pain point is that it is an emotional, not practical, need—a need for recognition, love, or reinforcement. Suppose you are selling health club memberships. For a prospect who is planning a trip to Hawaii in two months, the hot button could be losing a few pounds and looking good in a swimsuit. For a prospect who just found out they have high blood pressure, the hot button could be the health benefits of exercise. For a busy young mother, the hot button may

be the chance to get away from the kids for a few hours a week and reduce stress.

- *Eliminate objections.* When a prospect raises an objection, don't immediately jump in with a response. Instead, show empathy by saying "Let's explore your concerns." Ask for more details about the objection. You need to isolate the true objection so you can handle it. Here are some ways to do that:

    1. *Offer a choice.* "Is it the delivery time or the financing you are concerned about?"

    2. *Get to the heart of the matter.* "When you say you want to think about it, what specifically did you want to think about?"

    3. *Work toward a solution.* Every sale should be a win-win deal, which means one in which you both walk away feeling that you've done well. Therefore, you'll often need to compromise to close a deal: "I'll waive the shipping charge if you agree to the purchase."

    As you get more experience making sales calls, you'll become familiar with different objections. Maintain a list of common objections and ways you have successfully dealt with them.

TIP

Trying to scare up business? If your product isn't very appealing or exciting, one way to motivate customers is by describing the consequences of not using your product. For products that increase security or safety or improve health, fear can be an effective business-boosting tool.

- *Close the sale.* There is no magic to closing the sale. If you have followed all the previous steps, all you should have to do is ask for the customer's order. However, some sales-people make the mistake of simply not asking for the final decision. It's as if they forget their goal!

For some, "closing" sounds too negative. If you're one of them, try changing your thinking to something more positive, such as "deciding." As you talk with the customer, build in the close by having fun with it. Say something like "So how many do you want? We have it in a rainbow of colors; do you want them all?" Make sure to ask them several times in a fun, non-threatening way; you're leading them to make the decision.

After the Sale

- *Follow up*. What you do after the sale is as crucial as what you do to get it. "Nearly 85 percent of all sales are produced by word-of-mouth referrals," says sales expert Brian Tracy. "In other words, they're the result of someone telling a friend or associate to buy a product or service because the customer was satisfied." Concentrate on developing future and referral business with each satisfied customer. Write thank-you notes, call, or email customers after the sale to make sure they are satisfied, and maintain a schedule of future communications. Be in front of that client, and always show attention and responsiveness.

- *Ask for feedback*. Ask customers what you need to do to maintain and increase their business. This is often best done with an email in which they can respond to questions at their convenience and without the pressure of having someone waiting for a reply. Many customers have minor complaints but will never say anything. They just won't buy from you again. If you ask their opinions, on the other hand, they'll be glad to tell you—and, in most cases, will give you a chance to solve the problem. Feedback is important in any business—customer surveys can work wonders. Be careful not to give them just a handful of choices to respond to questions. Always leave a space for "other." You'd be surprised at how many answers don't fit your prepared survey. Give people an opportunity to add their own answers.

TIP

Sell benefits, not features. The biggest mistake entrepreneurs make is focusing on what their product or service is (its features). Rather, it's what it does (its benefits) that's important. A health-food product contains nutrients that are good for the body. That's what it is. What the product does is make the customer healthier, more energetic, and able to do more with less sleep.

Speaking Effectively

The difference between good and great salespeople is the way they deliver their messages. You can have the greatest sales pitch in the world, but if you deliver it with no enthusiasm, sincerity, or belief, you will lose the sale.

The Price Isn't Necessarily Right

How do you overcome that most common objection, "Your price is too high"? Lawrence L. Steinmetz and William T. Brooks, authors of *How to Sell at Margins Higher Than Your Competitors* (Wiley, 2005), say you need to learn how to acknowledge that your price is higher than competitors' and use that as a selling tool.

- Replace the idea of a higher price with a better value. This means giving customers more for their money: You offer a better quality of service, more services, better warranties, and/or higher-quality products for the extra cost, thus making the higher price seem less imposing.

- Whatever you do, don't be too willing to negotiate or slash prices, says Steinmetz.
- With the right ammunition, you can turn price problems into selling points.

Here are some suggestions to improve your speaking skills and power up your presentations:

- *Speak clearly.* If the prospect doesn't understand you, you won't get the sale.
- *Lean forward.* Leaning into the presentation gives the prospect a sense of urgency.
- *Don't fidget.* Knuckle-cracking, hair-twirling, and similar nervous habits detract from your presentation.
- *Don't "um," "ah," or "er."* These vocal tics are so irritating, they make the prospect focus on the flaws rather than the message. Best cure? Practice, practice, practice.
- *Be animated.* Act as if the best thing in the world just happened to you.
- *Vary your voice.* Don't drone on in a monotone. Punch the critical words. Go from high to low tones. Whisper some of the key information as if it's a secret. Get the prospect to lean into your words. Make them feel fortunate to be receiving this message.
- *Look prospects in the eye.* Eye contact signals credibility and trustworthiness.
- *Follow the prospect's lead.* Keep your tone similar to their tone.
- *Relax.* High anxiety makes prospects nervous. Why do salespeople get nervous? Either they are unprepared, or they need the money from the sale. Calm down. Never let them see you sweat.

Pass It On

Referrals are among a salesperson's best weapons. Yet many sales-people fail to take advantage of this powerful marketing tool. Here are secrets to getting and making the most out of referrals:

- *Make a list of people, groups, or organizations from whom you might get referrals.* Don't forget to include vendors and employ-ees.

- *Ask for specific referrals.* Many salespeople ask for referrals by saying "Do you know anyone else who might be interested in my products or services?" The prospect replies "Not off the top of my head, but I'll let you know if I think of anyone." And that's where it ends. More effective is to ask for a specific referral that deals with a need your business addresses. For instance, ask "Steve, at your last Rotary Club meeting, did you talk to anyone who was thinking about moving or selling a home?"

- *Gather as much information about the referral as possible.* Use this to prepare for your sales pitch.

- *Ask whomever referred you for permission to use their name when contacting the referral.*

- *Ask whomever referred you if they can help you get an appoint-ment with the referral.*

- *Contact the referral as soon as possible.*

- *Inform your customer about the outcome of the referral.* People like to know when they have been of help.

- *Prospect for referrals just as you would for sales leads.*

CHAPTER 8

Now Serving

Offering Superior Customer Service

TO THE ORDINARY ENTREPRENEUR, closing and finalizing the sale is the completion of serving the customer's needs. But for the pro, this is only the beginning. Closing the sale sets the stage for a relationship that, if properly managed by you, the entrepreneur, can be mutually profitable for years to come.

Remember the "80-20 rule"? The rule states that 80 percent of your business comes from 20 percent of your customers. Repeat customers are the backbone of every successful business. So now that you know how to land customers, it is time to learn how to keep them.

Building Customer Relationships

It's tempting to concentrate on making new sales or pursuing bigger accounts. But attention to your existing customers, no matter how small they are, is essential to keeping your business thriving. The secret to repeat business is following up in a way that has a positive effect on the customer.

TIP

To ensure you don't drop the ball on follow-up, check out one of the many contact management or sales software programs on the market. These little wonders can remind you of everything from a big client's birthday to an important sales call. Some will generate automatic—or personalized—emails for you.

Effective follow-up begins immediately after the sale when you call the customer to say "thank you" and find out if they are pleased with your product or service. Beyond this, there are several effective ways to follow up that ensure your business is always on the customer's mind:

- *Let customers know what you are working on for the future.* Post new product photos on your website, send emails, or start an enewsletter and include some of the things you have in store for the future that can benefit them.
- *Remember special occasions.* Send regular customers birthday cards, anniversary cards, holiday cards . . . you name it. Gifts are also excellent follow-up tools. You don't have to spend a fortune; use your creativity to come up with interesting gift ideas that tie into your business, the customer's business, or their recent purchase. If your business is relatively small, you can personalize the cards and even the gifts. In a larger business, you might personalize the cards and gifts for your biggest clients.
- *Pass on information.* If you read an article, see a new book, or hear about an organization that a customer might be interested in, shoot them an email letting them know you thought about them. Again, if your company is small this is easier to do. Otherwise, this can work for your most regular customers.
- *Consider follow-up calls.* When you talk to or visit old clients or customers, you'll often find they have referrals to give you, which can lead to new business.

With all that your existing customers can do for you, there's simply no reason not to stay in regular contact with them. Use your imagination, and you'll think of plenty of other ideas that can help you develop a lasting relationship.

FYI

Feeling alone? Wish you had someplace to advise you on better customer service? Try the International Customer Service Association's website (https://www.iccso.org/). You're required to join the organization to reap the benefits, but there are plenty of them—from networking opportunities to customer service training programs.

Customer Service

There are plenty of things you, the entrepreneur, can do to ensure good customer service. When you're a one-person business, it's easy to stay on top of what your customers want. But as you add employees, whether it's one person or 100, you are adding more links to the customer service chain—and creating more potential for poor service along the way.

That's why creating a customer service policy and adhering to it is so important. Here are some steps you can take to ensure that your clients receive excellent service every step of the way:

- Put your customer service policy in writing. These principles should come from you, but every employee should know what the rules are and be ready to live up to them.
- Establish support systems that give the employees clear instructions for gaining and maintaining service superiority. These systems will help you anticipate problems before they arise.
- Develop a measurement of superb customer service. Then reward employees who practice it consistently.
- Be certain that your passion for customer service runs throughout your company. Your employees should see how good service relates to your profits and to their future with the company.
- Be genuinely committed to providing more customer service excellence than anyone else in your industry. This

commitment must be so powerful that every one of your customers can sense it.

- Share information with people on the front lines. Meet regularly to talk about improving service. Solicit ideas from employees—they deal with the customers most often.
- Act on the knowledge that customers value attention, competence, promptness, and dependability. They love being treated as individuals and being referred to by name. (Don't you?)
- Empower customer service reps and salespeople with the ability to make decisions.

Walt Disney used to say that all your employees should be able to make decisions. And he was right: The last thing a customer wants to hear from an employee is "I'm sorry, only my manager can help you with this issue, and my manager isn't here."

Go to the Source

Excellent customer service is more than what you say or do for the customer; it also means giving customers a chance to make their feelings known. Here are some suggestions for finding out what your customers want, need, and care about:

- Attend trade shows and industry events that are important to your customers. You'll find out what the competition is doing and what kinds of products and services customers are looking for.
- Stay alert for trends; then respond to them. Read industry trade publications; be active in trade organizations; go online and learn what your customers are doing.
- Ask for feedback. Survey your customers regularly to find out how you're doing. Email a quick survey or have one on your website; set up focus groups or have a survey readily available in your store. Let customers know they can get a discount coupon from you as a thank you for filling out the short survey.

> • Ask for suggestions; then fix the trouble areas revealed.
>
> Whatever you do, don't rest on your laurels. Regularly evaluate your product or service to be sure it is still priced, packaged, and delivered right.

Interacting with Customers

Principles of customer service are nice, but you need to put those principles into action with everything you say and do. There are certain "magic words" that customers want to hear from you and your staff. Make sure all your employees understand the importance of these keywords:

- *"How can I help?"* Customers want the opportunity to explain in detail what they want and need. Too often, business owners feel the desire or the obligation to guess what customers need rather than carefully listening first. By asking how you can help, you begin the dialogue on a positive note. And by using an open-ended question, you invite discussion.
- *"I can solve that problem."* Most customers, especially B2B customers, are looking to buy solutions. They appreciate direct answers in a language they can understand.
- *"I don't know, but I'll find out."* When confronted with a difficult question that requires research on your part, admit it. Few things ruin your credibility faster than trying to answer a question when you are unsure of all the facts. An honest reply enhances your integrity.
- *"I will take responsibility."* Tell your customer you realize it's your responsibility to ensure a satisfactory outcome to the transaction. Assure the customer you know what she expects and will deliver the product or service at the agreed-upon price. There will be no unexpected expenses or changes required to solve the problem.

- *"I will keep you updated."* Even if your business is a cash-and-carry operation, it probably requires coordinating and scheduling numerous events. Assure your customers they will be advised of the status of these events. The longer your lead time, the more important this is. The vendors that customers trust the most are those that keep them apprised of the situation, whether the news is good or bad. And make sure you follow up with updates.

- *"I will deliver on time."* A due date that has been agreed on is a promise that must be kept. "Close" does not count. The first week in July means the first week in July, even though it contains a national holiday. Your clients are waiting to hear you say, "I deliver on time." The supplier who consistently does so is a rarity and well-remembered.

- *"It will be just what you ordered."* It will not be "similar to," and it will not be "better than" what was ordered. It will be exactly what was ordered. Even if you believe a substitute would be in the client's best interests, that's a topic for discussion, not something you decide on your own.

- *"The job will be completed."* Assure the customer there will be no waiting for a final piece or a last document. Never say you will be finished "except for . . ."

TIP

Join local community Facebook groups as well as surrounding communities, including those aimed at parents. Often, satisfied customers will recommend businesses on these groups. And as important, if someone has a complaint, you'll see the post and be able to act quickly to rectify it and avoid further word-of-mouth damage.

Complaint Department

Once upon a time dissatisfied customers rarely spoke up to let the merchant know they were unhappy. Today, there are places all over the internet to rate businesses and review them. People use websites like Yelp, Google, and many others to post either praise or complaints. Other sites like PissedConsumer.com are home to many complaints. And let's not forget the old standbys: ConsumerAffairs and the Better Business Bureau, both easily accessible online. Today, complaints can circulate widely across the web, and if it is something significant, become viral. This can destroy your credibility.

Even the best product or service meets with complaints or problems now and then. Here's how to handle them for positive results:

- Let customers vent their feelings. Encourage them to get their frustrations out in the open.
- Respond with an apology and explain why it should not have happened and what will be done in such situations going forward.
- Never argue with a customer. No, never.
- Never tell a customer "You do not have a problem." Those are fighting words.
- Share your point of view as politely as you can.
- Take responsibility for the problem. Don't make excuses. If an employee was sick or a third-party supplier let you down, that's not the customer's concern.
- Immediately take action to remedy the situation. Promising a solution then delaying it only makes matters worse.
- Empower your frontline employees to be flexible in resolving complaints. Give employees some leeway in deciding when to bend the rules. If you don't feel comfortable doing this, make sure they have you or another manager available to handle the situation at all times.
- Imagine you're the one with the complaint. How would you want the situation to be handled?

- *"I appreciate your business."* This means more than a simple "Thanks for the order." Genuine appreciation involves follow-up calls or emails, offering to answer questions, making sure everything is performing satisfactorily, and ascertaining that the original problem has been solved.

Neglecting any of these steps conveys the impression that you were interested in the person only until the sale was made. This leaves the buyer feeling deceived and used, and creates ill will and negative advertising for your company. Sincerely proving you care about your customers leads to recommendations and repeat sales.

TIP

When customers are happy with your service, ask them if they wouldn't mind giving you an online review. Get permission to use quotes from their online feedback on your site and in your brochures or other marketing pieces.

Going Above and Beyond

These days, simply providing adequate customer service is not enough. You need to go above and beyond the call of duty to provide customer service that truly stands out. How do you do this?

Begin by thinking about your own experiences as a customer— what you have liked and disliked in certain situations. Recall the times you were delighted by extra efforts taken to accommodate your needs or outraged by rudeness or negligence. This will give you greater insight into what makes for extraordinary customer service.

To put yourself in the customer's shoes, try visiting a wide range of businesses your customers are likely to frequent. This could include your direct competitors as well as companies that sell related products and services. Observe how customers are treated in addition to the kinds of services that seem to be important to them. Then adapt your business accordingly.

Keep in mind that good customer service is cost effective. Remind your staff that being polite, courteous, pleasant, and even smiling is simple.

Going above and beyond is especially important when a customer has complained or if there is a problem with a purchase. Suppose an order is delayed. What can you do?

- Call the customer personally with updates on the status of the order and expected arrival time.
- If you're in a small town or neighborhood, you could even hand-deliver the merchandise when it arrives.
- Take 20 or 30 percent off the cost.
- Send a note apologizing for the delay . . . tucked inside a gift basket full of goodies.

Of course, all these ideas depend on the size of the items. If someone orders major appliances and they arrive late, you need to put the above tips into action. If it's a matter of sending back the wrong side order with a food delivery, you can simply replace it or give them a discount next time they order from you.

AHA!

Create external incentives to keep customers coming back. Offer customers discounts, free inexpensive merchandise, or helpful services that can be added after they buy a certain amount. This gets them in the habit of buying again and again.

Going above and beyond doesn't always mean offering deep discounts or giving away products. With a little ingenuity and effort, you can show customers they are important at any time.

Suppose you've just received the newest samples and colors for your home furnishings line. Why not invite your best customers to a private showing, complete with music, appetizers, and a coupon good for one free hour of consultation?

Emergency orders and last-minute changes should be accommodated when possible, especially for important occasions such as a wedding or a big trade show. Customers remember these events and they will remember your flexibility and prompt response to their needs, too.

Customer loyalty is hard to win and easy to lose. But by going above and beyond with your customer service, you'll soon see your sales going above and beyond those of your competitors.

TIP

Learn from the best: Read about Zappos, the online shoe giant, and the amazing customer service for which they are known worldwide. Google "10 Things to Know About Zappos Customer Service" for a list of how the best of the best does it.

PART 3
Scaling

CHAPTER 9

Net Sales

Online Advertising and Marketing

IN 2020, ENTREPRENEURS SPENT OVER $365 BILLION on online marketing and advertising, which is an extraordinary amount when you consider that just $8.11 billion was spent on television advertising. Clearly, business owners are well aware that people are not only shopping on their laptops or notebooks, but millions of folks are also browsing and buying on their cell phones as well. As a result, smart entrepreneurs know the power of the internet to present, promote, and sell almost anything their audience could possibly want to purchase. The question is no longer: Should I do my marketing and advertising on the internet? Instead, it's what's the best way to use the internet to boost my sales?

A Marketing Tool

Your website as well as your presence on social media platforms like Facebook and LinkedIn should be used as marketing tools to attract a wide or narrow target audience, depending on what you are selling and who you are looking to sell it to. Your job is to attract people to your business through your web presence. If your website or social media posts talk only about your company and how great you are, chances are no one will be interested. If, however, you use lead magnets (things that excite people and make them return for more), you can increase sales significantly.

Savvy marketers master permission marketing, which means

marketing that gives users the chance to choose what they want to learn more about as opposed to what is thrown at them by spammers, scammers, and others who choose to abuse the system. For example, let's say you run the Clicks and Bricks Bed and Breakfast in Vermont. Spring and fall are your off-seasons. You'd like to reach out to former visitors and those who have sent emails inquiring about the Clicks and Bricks B&B.

Using the principles of permission marketing, you can:

- Use your database of customer and prospect emails to build an audience for a promotional campaign.
- Recognize that those consumers have indicated an interest in talking with you or exploring your website further. So tempt them with an offer of "three nights for the price of two" or run a contest on your site for a free two-night midweek stay. It's offers like these that keep customers and prospects engaged.
- Encourage a learning relationship with your customers. Send emails about upcoming local events, such as the annual Scenic Fall Photo Festival, or offer two-for-one coupons for an upcoming art show. Remind them of Vermont's allure in the spring and fall.
- Deepen your communication as site visitors become customers and first-timers become return visitors. Send birthday or anniversary cards. Reward them with deals that not only bring them to your B&B but offer additional value, like skiing in the winter or nature walks in the warmer months.

Now think about how you might be able to apply these examples to your own business. How can you think creatively to boost your permission marketing outreach efforts?

Attracting Visitors to Your Site

With millions of websites out there, attracting visitors to your site is often the biggest challenge. The real question is, once you've got the site up and going, how do you get people to your site with so much competition out there? Your strategies for doing so may include search engines, paid search services, and affiliates. Let's consider them one at a time.

Search Engines and Rankings

Search engines have become a ubiquitous part of American culture. Every day millions of Americans go online to search the internet or google something or someone. Web searching is the primary point of discovery for most of us, especially when we are seeking new products or services. So how do you get noticed? Perhaps the most important—and inexpensive—strategy for getting people to your website is to rank high for your preferred keywords on the main search engines in "organic" or "natural" searches (as opposed to paid ads, also known as sponsored links).

Search engines (Google, Yahoo!, Bing, etc.) use different criteria for rankings. Along with keywords in the text, as well as meta titles and descriptions, Searchmetrics, a digital marketing analytics company, lists several other areas of focus when trying to boost your website ranking. These include: backlinks, a sitemap, internal linking, the URL structure, site speed, how long visitors spend on each page, how much traffic your site is getting, and how current the pages are. These are some among a variety of factors that may weigh in on search ranking.

Among other components, achieving a high rank is often based on three criteria: competition, relevancy, and content. Think of "competition" like popularity. The more popular (talked about, linked to, and clicked on) your offer or website is, the more competitive you are. "Relevancy" is based on how well your offer or site matches the keywords. Your site should include the keywords, or be as close as possible to the keywords that are being searched. Finally, your "content" should address the question being asked. Your goal is to answer the query as directly as possible. You want the end user to say "Yes, this is the answer I'm looking for." The sooner you master these three criteria, the higher rank you'll be able to achieve in search results. Mastering the art of search is not impossible; it just takes practice, time, and consistency. Take the time to think about what your potential customers are really asking and how your offer or website answers their questions. Be persistent and consistent, work through the learning curve, and you'll find yourself with a high rank in the search engines. Keep in mind, however, that the learning curve changes—for example, several years ago mobility was not as significant as it is today, since so many people are searching from their cell phones.

TIP

Remember keywords are one of your best strategies for successful marketing. Think of all the keywords and phrases for your product or service—those words and phrases that people will enter into a search. You want to make sure you include them in your title page, meta description tags, body content, header tags and subheads, and outgoing links. You should also include keywords have it in your domain name, which is typically your business name. For example, the domain name for Derek's Auto Repair is dereksautorepair.com, with the keywords "auto repair" included, so that when someone searches for auto repairs, Derek's auto shop will be among the results. Be careful, however, not to overdo it or make it blatant that you are packing keywords into your content. Search engines are programmed to know that you are overdoing it and will downgrade your ranking.

There are many search engines out there, and they all differ in structure, search strategy, and efficiency. However, Google continues to dominate the global search engine market share in 2023. It accounts for over 90% of all searches worldwide. As of May 2023, 93.12% of all search queries conducted across all search engine providers were done through Google. Even with innovations like Microsoft's Bing using GPT-4, it has not gained significant market share.

For the best exposure, be sure your website is listed on Google. Also don't forget other players like Bing and Yahoo!. And when using keywords, remember it's important to have them appear naturally. You can check Google Ads and Google Insights to get a good idea of what sort of words and phrases people search for in your category.

TIP

The easiest way to get ranked on search engines in 2023 includes several key strategies and tactics, including the following:

- Optimize for Google's E-EAT Algorithm by focusing on demonstrating Experience, Expertise, Authority, and Trust in content to rank higher
- Consider looking into utilizing artificial intelligence (AI) to stay ahead of competitors and align with technological advancements
- Optimize for Google RankBrain, using long-tail keywords to find link-building opportunities
- With Google Discover targeting mobile phone users, optimizing your website for mobile can provide higher visibility
- Ensure fast-loading, high-performing websites because speed and performance have become critical in 2023 for user satisfaction and rankings

There are some good online tools you can use to compare yourself with the competition including:

- *semrush.com*: This all-in-one digital marketing platform is highly regarded for competitor research, SEO, content marketing, and more.
- *BuzzSumo.com*: This tool is ideal for competitive research in content and is also useful for SEO.
- *iSpionage.com:* Shows you how you compare to your competitors in terms of search traffic.

Keep in mind that Google's share of search is so significant that it's important to spend the most time refining your keywords for Google success.

Also keep in mind that the narrower the category, the better your chance of scoring unique visitors; for example, "percussion instruments" and "ice skating dresses" are more specific than "drums" and "sports attire" and have a better chance of scoring clicks. Think about how specific you might get when searching for an item and apply it to your business.

TIP

Having a blog on your website can not only help drive traffic to the site and increase the number of return visitors, but it can help you in your search engine rankings. They can be short (200 to 300 words) or long (1,000 words) and vary in frequency, but consider running one on your site weekly, twice monthly, or monthly.

"Many a small thing has been made large by the right kind of advertising."
—Mark Twain

The cost of your Google Ads campaign depends on how much you're willing to pay and how well you know your audience. It all boils down to knowing your goals and letting Google know what they are. Google will grant the highest position to the advertiser with the highest keywords bid and the highest clickthrough rate. According to Google, your ad's position on the page is determined by your ad rank. You can find more insight and tips for boosting your ad's position at support.google.com/google-ads.

In the Microsoft Advertising (formerly Bing Ads) program, you aren't charged to create an account; you only pay when someone clicks on your ad. The highest position is given to the advertiser with the highest keywords bid and the highest clickthrough rate. You can budget by the day or by the overall campaign goal, and the automated metrics will help manage your result. You will gain further insight into who turns into a customer once they click. Bing claims that it can reach some audiences Google doesn't and that 27 percent of its clicks come from searches exclusive to Bing. The bulk of all searches, however, still come from Google.

Local Search

Want local customers to find you? Then try local search engine advertising, which lets you target ads to a specific state, city, or even neighborhood. A growing number of small businesses are using local search.

Like other search engine advertising, the local variety lets you track your account closely to find out which keywords are most successful at drawing customers and how much you're spending each day. Local search ads on Google or other search engines offer local search options. This helps people find what is nearby when they search for things such as "nearest restaurant" or "coffee near me." The benefit of local search is bringing more local traffic to your business. You can also provide basic, yet important, information, such as store hours, location, customer reviews, and if there is a special offer or deal going on.

TIP

More than 60 percent of consumers search for products and services on their mobile devices, according to a 2020 report from Hitwise, a service that provides data on trends in visitor and search behavior. Certain sectors of the market trend much higher, such as food and beverage, which checks in at 72 percent mobile searches. You can use either paid search engines or display mobile advertising companies, such as AdMob (now owned by Google, admob.google.com; Smaato (smaato.com/), or InMobi (inmobi.com/). Image and text requirements for mobile ads through these and other companies, as well as through Google Ads, differ from desktop ads, so be sure to understand the difference so you can maximize your reach.

Affiliates

Firms that sell products and services on their websites for commissions offer another way to draw site visitors. The web is democratic—a SOHO (small office/home office) can be an affiliate of a Fortune 500 firm, as can other corporate giants, midsize businesses, and even charities.

Affiliates place merchant promotions on their websites to sell goods or services. They control the type of promotion, location on the site, and the length of time it runs. In return, the affiliate earns commission on clickthroughs, leads, or purchases made through the site. For example, your town's Big Bank could be the affiliate looking for local merchants to advertise on its site. It has a restaurant, an office supply store, a realtor, a law firm, and an accounting firm with ads or promotions on its site. Depending on what they negotiated with Big Bank, these businesses will pay commissions on sales that initiated from the bank's website. For every clickthrough that results in a sale, affiliates can earn a commission from 1 to 10 percent for multichannel retailers or 30 to 50 percent in the software sector.

You may want to consider joining an affiliate program network, which provides all the tools and services affiliates and merchants need to create, manage, and optimize successful affiliate marketing programs. Sites that offer quality programs include Rakuten Advertising (rakutenadvertising.com/affiliate)—which has offered deals with Sam's Club, Old Navy, and Lowe's among other major brands—and CJ Affiliate by Conversant (cj.com). Another route is using your favorite search engines to find companies that have potential as affiliates. For example, if you own a gym and sell workout products, you might want to affiliate with nutritionists, personal trainers, sports drinks, vitamin, and health-food partners. If you decide to run your own affiliate program, Keap (keap.com) offers a complete email marketing system and everything you'll need to run a successful affiliate program.

Calling All Followers

When it comes to marketing anything on social media, without a large following, you most likely won't get very far. Getting there can be hard, but R.L. Adams, an entrepreneur and software engineer, offers these three tips for making the journey to a larger footprint.

1. *Define your niche audience.* Who are you targeting? Get specific. This is important because you'll be curating your content toward that intended audience. Everything you do or say should be geared toward this audience or demographic. The more you can define your demographic, the higher your chances for success.

2. *Add massive value.* You can't succeed on social media without adding massive amounts of value. There's fierce competition in the marketplace, and the stakes are high. Find ways you can share your expertise with others, as well as help the people that follow you in some way. The more you focus on this mentality, the more likely you'll be to succeed in the long run.

3. *Collaborate.* Find like-minded entrepreneurs on social media with whom you can collaborate. Reach out to them. Build a group or find another way that you can team up with others who might be in a similar situation as yourself or with a similar number of followers. There is power in numbers. You can't expect to do this yourself or go it alone. Give accolades and praise to others and form joint ventures with other people if you want to see sustained growth in followers and fans over time.

FYI

Want to know more about search engines? Search Engine Watch (searchenginewatch.com) can answer your questions. It compares the major search engines and tells you how to get listed. It also provides tips for searches so you can learn to think like your customers and make it easier for them to find you. Plus, you can sign up for a free newsletter.

Keeping Visitors on Your Site

A good website design and strategy for attracting visitors takes you three-quarters of the way to success. The final step is getting people to try your offerings and come back for more. The best way to do that is to treat each customer as unique. Fortunately, the web lends itself to the kind of personalization that's relatively easy and inexpensive for even the smallest business.

With a little effort, you can address each site visitor's needs effectively. Combined with offline strategic work—such as hitting customers every other week with a free newsletter or offering them a two-for-one special if they haven't visited your site in two months—readily available ecommerce tools enable you to personalize your site to meet the needs of your customers.

The basis for customization is the cookie—a morsel of information that lets sites know where customers go. A cookie is a piece of data that's sent to the browser along with an HTML page when someone visits a site. The browser saves the cookie to the visitor's hard drive. When that customer revisits the site, the cookie goes back to the web server along with the customer's new request, enabling your site to recognize the return visitor. It's Important to note that Google has decided to phase out third-party cookies by 2024 so depending on when you are reading this, they may already be eliminated.

Here are some ideas for marketing programs you can create from an analysis of stored cookies and email:

- Send an email to customers who haven't bought anything from your site in three months, offering a $10 or $20 reward for shopping online.
- Send an email with a new promotion a few weeks or months after a customer makes a purchase.
- Offer a chance to win something and make it easy for visitors who drop in at least once a week to enter the contest.

If personalization seems too complicated, you can still design your website to speak to different groups of people. Let's say you're a realtor wanting your site to meet several needs. Create a screen with a menu that includes options for buyers, sellers, other realtors, or up and coming realtors who simply want to apply to work at your company. Each user can then be directed to a page that meets their reason for visiting your site. And don't forget the "About Us" page, where people can simply find out more about your business—who you are, how long you've been in business, and what type of real estate you sell.

Getting visitors to stick around long enough to explore your site is just as important as tempting them to visit in the first place. Here are some tips on capturing your visitors' attention:

- *Make connections.* Hyperlink your email address; this means most visitors can simply click to open a blank message and send you a note.
- *Have fun.* People who surf the internet are looking for fun, entertainment, or distraction from their day-to-day routines. You don't have to be wild and wacky (unless you want to be). Just make sure you offer original content presented in an entertaining way.
- *Add value.* Offering something useful that customers can do adds tremendous value to your site. For example, customers can track their own packages at the FedEx or UPS site or concoct a recipe for a new drink at the Tito's vodka site. While it doesn't have to be quite so elaborate, offering users the ability to download forms, play games, or create something useful or fun will keep them coming back.
- *Keep it simple.* Don't build a site that's more than three or four levels deep. Internet users love to surf, but they get bored when they have to sift through loads of information to find what they're looking for.
- *Provide a map.* Use icons to create clear navigational paths. A well-designed site should have a button at the bottom of each subpage that transports the visitor back to the site's homepage.
- *Stage a contest.* Nothing is more compelling than giving something away. Have the contestants fill out a registration form so you can find out who's coming to your site.
- *Make payment a snap.* If you're setting up an online storefront, give customers an easy and quick way to pay you. Accept payment options like PayPal and set up shipping costs that are simple and can be added to the final sales total instantly.
- *Update your site often.* New content, new offers, new photos, new blogs, new giveaways—do whatever you can to make sure the visitors will always find something new and of interest on your site.

Use these tips to get started on the road to offering an engaging, welcoming site that will keep your visitors coming back.

The Ad-Free Zone

When you design your website's marketing plan, remember that the internet is a community with its own set of rules that you as an entrepreneur must understand to be successful. The primary rule is: Don't send spam.

Reach Out and Email Someone

The Direct Marketing Association offers some practical advice on how to be more successful at reaching current and potential customers through email:

- Encourage customers and prospects to add your email address to their personal "approved list/address book." Being an "approved" sender yields higher response rates and generates fewer complaints and blocking issues.
- Carefully consider the content and presentation of your marketing messages because recipients are increasingly labeling any email communication that's not relevant or looks suspicious as spam.
- Click the "spam check" button in your email program to see if your email is at risk for being marked as spam. Most ISPs use spam-filtering software. This technology uses algorithms to determine whether incoming messages qualify as junk email and filters them out before they get to a client's inbox. In addition, you should register for all mailbox provider feedback loops. In general, aim to keep complaint rates (total complaints divided by total delivered email) below 0.1 percent to avoid temporary or long-term blockages.
- Adopt good list-hygiene and list-monitoring practices that help facilitate message delivery. Monitoring campaign delivery as well as open and clickthrough rates is essential because low open rates or high bounce-back rates may indicate a delivery problem.

Way back in 2004, the CAN-SPAM Act of 2003 was signed into law. It set forth the first national standards for governing commercial email. The law requires commercial email messages to be labeled and to include opt-out instructions as well as the sender's physical address. It also prohibits the use of deceptive subject lines and false headers. A good way to get folks to opt in to your email list—which of course they'll have the option of opting out of—is to offer a free monthly email enewsletter or a similar incentive, such as being the first to receive info on upcoming sales or special offers.

Content is wide open, but effective enewsletters usually mix news about trends in your field with tips and updates on sales or special pricing. Include hyperlinks so interested readers can, with a single click of the mouse, go directly to your site and find out more about a topic of interest.

Another tip to keep in mind: Don't post commercial messages to newsgroups that have rules against these types of messages. For example, on the social networking site LinkedIn, don't post messages that sound like sales pitches to any of the groups. However, if you're offering valuable content and resources or if you're looking to start a discussion on a topic, keep it fairly broad so many people can join in, and then by all means, post away.

FYI

You can get more detailed info about the CAN-SPAM Act and how it might affect your business by visiting the Federal Trade Commission's info site. You can find it quickly by doing a search on FTC CAN-SPAM Act.

CHAPTER 10

Social Media

Using Online Platforms
to Spread the Word

SOCIAL MEDIA HAS BECOME A NECESSARY TOOL to connect and engage with your audience—and in today's marketing landscape, that's how brands are built.

Social media marketing is simply using social sites, such as Facebook, LinkedIn, Snapchat, Instagram, Twitter, and YouTube, to market your business—and, when possible, to create a community of people excited about your brand. This marketing medium is more demanding on businesses because to promote and build a brand, you must engage in conversations with your target market.

The "2023 Social Media Marketing Industry Report," by researcher Michael Stelzner of Social Media Examiner, shows that 86 percent of all marketers indicated that their social media efforts have generated more exposure for their businesses. The second major benefit was increased traffic, with businesses reporting 76 percent positive reports.

Blogging

One of the most powerful tools you can include on your website is a blog, which is essentially a short article that talks directly to your audience. The word "blog" is derived from the term "web log," which is an ongoing summary (log) maintained by an individual who regularly enters commentary, descriptions of events, or other material.

One of the reasons for having a weekly, bimonthly, or monthly blog is that websites can become static and dated. In addition, websites are sometimes not very interactive, which means you're not engaging or talking with your customers or clients. Putting a blog on your website allows you to engage in a two-way conversation with your market. To start the conversation, you can post valuable content, including tips, anecdotes, industry insights, commentary, and/or reviews in your blog.

Blogging, which dates to the early '90s, gained popularity quickly, and today, it is one of the most powerful interactive tools on the net. Whether you already have a blog or you need to set one up, there's one thing you need to do . . . become active as a blogger or hire someone to write it for you.

TIP

Images can make a huge difference in how customers interact with and view a brand. About 90 percent of information that is sent to the brain is visual. According to research by CrowdRiff, a marketing firm that focuses on visual impact, 60 percent of customers are more likely to consider a business with images appearing in local search. And while the average person will read only 20 percent of the words on a web page, they'll look at every image. A full 67 percent of customers said images were important in making a purchasing decision. Facebook posts with images see 2.3 times more engagement than those without them, according to BuzzSumo. The takeaway: Use engaging, appropriate images to keep customers interested in what you post on social media. Hint: Use your smartphone to get real images rather than generic-looking stock photos.

According to lead generation website OptinMonster, there are roughly 409 million people each month viewing over 20 billion pages. In addition, there are some 77 million new blog comments generated by readers every month. It's been estimated that the average blog post takes 3.5 hours to write. So get started, if you are not already blogging.

The key to building readers and followers for your blog is to be active and post valuable and compelling information on a regular basis. Serious bloggers post and market their blogs on social media sites daily. Although this is a powerful and effective way to build readers and followers, daily posting isn't necessary to grow your blog. All you need to do is allocate posting time that fits within your marketing schedule—and stick to it. Consistency is key when you launch and operate a blog. Your readers will begin to expect and look forward to your posts. Be sure to optimize your blog for mobile, as a great majority of people view the internet from smartphones and tablets.

The first thing you need to do is find a blog platform. A blog platform is a site that allows you to set up, design, and even host your blog. Most are free, although some offer upgrade capabilities and options.

AHA!

Google Alerts are a great way to keep track of buzz and conversations happening about you and your company. Go to google.com/alerts and enter your company name and any keywords that might come up in a conversation about your brand. Whenever something is posted on the internet with those keywords, Google will send you an email with the link. You can set this up to keep an eye on your competitors, too.

A few top blog platforms include:

- WordPress: wordpress.com
- Network Solutions: networksolutions.com
- Blogger: blogger.com/start, a Google platform

- Wix: wix.com
- Medium: medium.com

Most web creation tools and sites will also allow you to plug in a blog, either by building it from the host site or by including a widget that links readers back to one of these blog-specific platforms. It's up to you to make it as fancy or simple as you like—and as your time allows.

Video Marketing

Just as marketing has evolved, so has the internet. What started as static, text-heavy sites have evolved into interactive and informative video pages. According to researcher E2M Solution's "Demand Generation" survey, 92 percent of marketers used video to leverage demand, more than any other type of lead generation effort online. There's a reason for that: 80 percent of the respondents in the "Demand Generation" study say they prefer interactive content. The more fun, humorous, and engaging they are, the more likely they will become viral, contends Mike Koenigs, serial entrepreneur and founder of website traffic generation site Traffic Geyser.

You may also want to consider a video blog (aka vlog), because people respond well to videos. This can include stories, tips, customers talking about your products and/or services, as well as demonstrations of what your products or services can do to meet the needs of your customers. Plan videos in advance, and rehearse, then edit carefully. Videos can benefit your business, but great videos can go viral and catapult your business. It's also important that you are careful and sensitive regarding what you post on your videos and that you have signed permission to put other people in them.

One of the quickest, most affordable ways to create a video is to use a smartphone and record short videos for your target market. They don't have to be fancy; they just have to be fun and informative. A quick and easy way to launch a video campaign and make it go viral is to create short video clips of two to three minutes in length that feature frequently asked and answered questions from your customers. People are most likely to leave a video if they're not captivated in the first ten seconds, explains Danny Donchev, an SEO expert and author. Short videos are a great option if your goal is to get an immediate reaction from viewers, like when you are offering a limited-time deal that requires them to act quickly.

TIP

According to Google, almost 50 percent of internet users look for videos related to a product or service before visiting a store. In addition, according to Jack Shepherd of the Social Shepherd blog, there was an estimated 3.37 billion internet users consuming video content in 2022. Consider making even a simple how-to or promotional video about your product or service and post it to your website.

Overview of Social Bookmarking Sites

Traffic from social bookmarking sites can give your site a huge boost in traffic, delivering thousands of visitors in just a few hours. While the initial effects can be temporary, if you give people a reason to come back to your website, you'll certainly notice a positive cumulative effect.

What is social bookmarking, how does it work, how can you get people to bookmark you, and what can you expect? Social bookmarking is an online service that allows members to add page links as bookmarks, categorize those links, and provide added commentary. These bookmarks are then made available to the other community members who are also generally allowed to make their own comments on the bookmarked page.

The service that kicked off the social bookmarking craze in

2003 was Del.icio.us. Since that time, hundreds of other social bookmarking services have been launched, with the most popular being Pinterest (pinterest.com), Digg (digg.com/), Reddit (reddit.com), Twitter (twitter.com), and Mix (mix.com). All these services have the ability to deliver hundreds or thousands of targeted visitors to your site within a very short time, sometimes within hours of your page having been bookmarked if the wider community finds the entry of interest.

To make sharing content easier, consider adding ShareThis tools to your site found at ShareThis.com. They have icons that make it easy to share ideas, articles, and content online. They have great tools to increase traffic and engagement, and with one click, visitors can share your content with all their online networks.

AHA!

By posting and/or retweeting links, articles, news stories, and any readable content, you are in effect bookmarking it for later use. You can then revisit your account later to wade through your social saves.

Content Marketing Online

You can harness the power of content marketing by writing short articles related to your respective industry and posting online, either on your own social network platforms, such as LinkedIn, or perhaps on a website in your industry—find out who handles content for the site and see if they would be interested. Each article should include a bio box and byline that includes references and contact information for the author's business. Well-written content articles released for free distribution have the potential of increasing the credibility of the business, as well as attracting new clients.

If writing is not your forte and you're worried about creating powerful articles or content, there are hundreds of sites that offer writing services, such as thewritersforhire.com or Upwork (upwork.com), where you can set a budget for a project and post the job for hire. You could also engage with Contently (contently.com) to produce material, or simply search for freelance bloggers or writers in your area. Remember, this is your business, and people will be learning about you and your business through the blog posts, so skimping on things like content is a bad idea. Marketing Insider Group points out that a blog post could cost you $5 to $50 for a poorly written one, or up to $1,000 for content from top bloggers. Truth is, there are a wide range of prices, but you can usually get a good quality blog post for $150 to $300. Remember, the value isn't in spending the least amount of money, it's getting something back for your dollars, like readers who become paying customers in this case.

With the advent of artificial intelligence (AI) content generation tools, some business owners and content writers are using experimenting with tools like jasper.ai or ChatGPT (openai.com/blog/chatgpt). You may wish to investigate their use for your own business.

TIP

Post articles to chosen sites and link back to your blog, client, or marketing campaign site. Make sure to include tags and keywords relevant to your content topic when posting. Develop a list of relevant industry blogs, enewsletters, and Twitter feeds, and send your link to those, too. Post your most insightful blog content to LinkedIn.

Words Heard Round the World

Here are a few quick tips on how to take an article and make it viral online:

- *Post on discussion boards and forums.* Post snippets of your article or the article title in forums and on discussion boards that are related to your target market or topic focus. Don't forget to include your full name and website or blog URL where the article is located.

- *Compile articles into an ebook.* Compile the articles into an ebook that you can use for lead generation. For example, if you own a gym and want to get more people in to work out, offer an ebook featuring short articles and anecdotes about how to motivate yourself to get to the gym and to do a regular routine. Distribute the ebooks via your website and/or on your email list. Give your readers the right to distribute them as well. This is viral marketing at work. If your ebook is for sale, offer to share revenue if readers distribute it to their list and you make a sale. This is called an affiliate marketing program.

- *Write a variety of articles.* The trick to reaching a massive amount of people is to create a variety of articles. For example, if you want to promote your public relations service, you could post content on how to write an article, how to come up with eye-catching headlines, what makes an article jump off the page, or how and where to distribute the articles.

- *Add a disclosure at the end or bottom of each article.* Your disclosure statement should say something like this: "This article may be freely reprinted or distributed in its entirety in any, newsletter, blog, or website." Then make sure it has your name (or the author's name if someone else wrote it), a brief byline about the author, and web links. Add that the "author's name, byline, and link must remain intact and be included with all reproductions."

Another great analytics tool you can use to track where visitors are coming from, what article pages they visit on your site, and how long they stay is Google Analytics. It's a free service and fairly simple to set up. Go to google.com/analytics to set up an account. The analytics site offers a complete tutorial; however, if you're still unsure how to use it, you can ask a web programmer to set it up for you in a matter of minutes.

Social Marketing Automation

With all the social site tools available, often the best way to be effective with your social marketing is to automate the process. First, you need to decide whether automation is right for you and, if so, which automation you should set up. Automation can be key in turning your contacts into profits because you can post less, but at the same time, you get more exposure. Social automation, however, can be considered spamming, so be careful with how you set it up.

How does social network automation work? By using tools like Hootsuite (hootsuite.com) and SocialFlow (socialflow.com) to automate your social networking sites, these sites can submit a link or post to not just one or two sites but, in some cases, up to 60. Sometimes, though, the link posted isn't relevant for the site it goes out to. In other words, the links aren't even relevant for the members of the network, and sometimes they're not properly tagged or categorized. This eventually leads to negative votes on the article or post submitted, so make sure you set up your automation properly.

Meet the Expert: Mike Allton, Social Media Guru

Mike Allton is an award-winning blogger, speaker, an author at The Social Media Hat, and Brand Evangelist at Agorapulse where he strengthens relationships with social media educators, influencers, and agencies. Allton is also the co-author of the *Ultimate Guide to Social Media Marketing* (Entrepreneur Press, 2020) alongside Jenn Herman, Stephanie Liu, Amanda Robinson, and Eric Butow.

Social media can seem daunting for small-business owners. How do you recommend getting started with a content strategy?

First, small-business owners should understand that they do not have to post every day, but also that social media is how you can stand out and engage your customers on a personal level. Next, consider your strengths in terms of content creation. Do you like to write or take pictures or do you love to shoot video? What will be easiest? What might work best for your type of business and target audience? Armed with that information, select the most appropriate social network for that kind of content and then focus on that platform.

What is the most important factor to consider when figuring out what platforms to use?

If you've homed in on a particular type of content, that will narrow which platforms to use, but will still leave several to choose from since platforms like Facebook and LinkedIn support all kinds of content. So think next about your brand tone of voice, style, and your target audience. If you're a professional B2B brand, LinkedIn may be your best bet, while a B2C brand focused on younger consumers may look to Instagram or TikTok. Which means that, after determining the type of content you can create, the most important factor is platform demographic.

How can small businesses get the most bang for their buck with social media?

Go live. The most powerful medium a business can use is live video. You can broadcast to most platforms, even multiple platforms simultaneously, and use live video to create real connections with your audience. They will see and hear you and if they comment on your video, you can engage with them real-time. And once your video has concluded, you can use the recording to create short snippets for other platforms or even long-form written content for your blog. A small business that broadcasts just one live video a week can spin that into dozens and dozens of other pieces of content.

What makes a social strategy successful? How do you measure success?

What does success look like? That's the first question every business needs to answer for themselves. That could be sales or traffic or leads or brand awareness. For most brands, social media is best suited for building brand awareness and community, which can then be measured in terms of reach, group members, engagement, email subscribers, or even ambassadors. Tools like Agorapulse, for instance, can automatically identify people who engage with and regularly share a brand's social posts and content and flag them as friends and ambassadors.

What is the role of content in a small biz social strategy? Are there types of content that work better than others on various platforms?

Content can play many, many roles for businesses, but where small businesses can benefit most is through creating bottom of funnel content: articles that help prospects compare and contrast and, ultimately, decide to buy from a business. When those articles exist in a brand's archive, savvy social media managers can pay attention to conversations and questions that come up on social, even outside of their own company posts, and find opportunities to share links to resources. While I tend to prefer long-form blog content, videos, ebooks, podcasts, infographics, and other kinds of content can all work well to varying degrees, depending on the target audience and their experience.

- *Link your blog to LinkedIn.* Go to "Applications" and click on "WordPress" if you have a WordPress blog, or go to "Applications," then "Blog Link" if you have a TypePad blog. LinkedIn will walk you through the process step by step—and it does change the process sometimes, so check before you attempt to link your blog.
- *Link your blog to Twitter.* Dlvr.it (dlvrit.com) is a handy, free website and application that will "feed your blog to Twitter." Go to dlvrit.com, sign up for an account, verify, and log in, then click the "Create New Feed" button, and add

your blog. It might take a couple of hours to start working, but once it's going, it's fairly reliable unless Twitter goes down or has API issues. Check the stream once a week. You can also use this service to link your blog to other social media as well.

- *Use a service like Hootsuite, where you can schedule posts months in advance.* You can also use the service to link to all your social media accounts, from Twitter and Facebook to LinkedIn and even Pinterest. Your most popular articles or blog posts can be "socialed" months into the future to give them new life. Just be sure to make it clear that they're older posts (add the phrase "In case you missed it," or "ICYMI" in Twitterspeak).

The Human Connection

There are some common problems with social media automation. First, there is the reality that your posts can sound mechanical or lacking in human engagement. Social media has a give and take, in which people are communicating. Interacting in real time provides the human element that is often lacking in automation. While you can automate your own content to be posted on certain days or nights at specific times anyplace in the world, third-party content is often promoted by the website with whom you have teamed up, such as saying "posted by Hootsuite." This takes away the human connection that social media is all about.

Another way to automate your blog so it posts to the social sites you're active on is to set up widgets and add plug-ins. You can do this for sites like Twitter, Facebook, LinkedIn, YouTube, Digg, and many more. The way a widget works is every time you post on one social site it will go out to your blog as an update. First, you need to make sure your blog allows widgets. Some blogs won't allow widgets unless you host the blog on your own site. Once you determine whether you can add these widgets, log in to each of the sites you want to add a widget to, go to the search box and type in "widget," and that will take you to the most current directions on how to upload or generate the HTML code needed to post widgets to your blog.

Plug-ins are applications that can enhance the capabilities of your blog, such as the All in One SEO plug-ins available on Word-Press, which helps you optimize your blog for search engines and mobile viewing. Thousands of plug-ins are available.

Keep in mind that while automation can make sure your content is posted on a prearranged schedule, it can become too easy to forget you have it running. By not keeping a careful watch on the automated posts, you could ruin your reputation. For example, an automated post that praises a product that has been recalled the day before could be embarrassing and damaging to your reputation. Monitor your postings.

CHAPTER 11

Can You Relate?

Social Media Networking

IN THE PAST FIVE YEARS, connecting on social networking sites has rocketed from a niche activity into a phenomenon that engages tens of millions of internet users.

According to Statista, the number of worldwide active social media users is expected to increase from 3.6 billion in 2020 to over 4.4 billion by 2025.

Through the early years of this social movement, this approach to networking was overlooked as a marketing vehicle for business owners. That has changed radically, although some small businesses have yet to take full advantage of social media communities in a meaningful way.

High-Level Networking

When networking online, you need to be efficient with your time and even more effective with whom you choose to connect with. It's important to know how to choose the people with whom you'll connect online. There are two different types of networkers online—the posters and the seekers. Your business is a poster, which means you actively post valuable information, resources, tips, and offers. The seekers are your customers—they're actively seeking your products and services. You'll find seekers in discussion areas, forums, groups, and engaging on fan pages.

When searching for quality contacts to use online for networking, start with connection sites, such as LinkedIn, and look for high-level networkers (HLN). You'll know an HLN when you see one; they're active online, have at least 500 connections, and have powerful profiles, which means their profiles are set up completely and leave out little-to-no information. Make sure these contacts have at least one of the three criteria before you connect with them online. Some examples of HLNs are decision makers, executives, the media, and the movers and shakers in your industry. Don't let the fact that you don't yet know the person hold you back from sending an invite to connect. Simply be transparent, and let them know why you'd like to connect with them online. Whether you're offering your help, sending them a resource, or introducing them to one of your connections, make sure you make it about how you can help them and not how they can help you.

FYI

Check out Meetup.com, an online networking site that facilitates offline networking. Members can create and join groups of people with similar interests who live in their area, and they can easily organize real-life meetings. It's a great way to meet potential business partners and clients. It's usually free to participate in monthly meetup events, although some events come with a nominal organization fee or participation cost.

Target Market Connections

Target market connections (TMCs) are a group of consumers at which your company aims its products and services. They're found by using keywords in the search section on social media sites, as well as in groups and discussion areas in your area of interest or focus. TMCs are mostly seekers that chat and seek out information by posting questions online. In the most basic terms, they're seeking you. The key is to join in the groups and discussions where your target market is talking and engage with them. But remember, engaging doesn't mean selling—if you become a pushy salesperson, you will not make many connections. You can also send them an invite to connect and let them know that you sent them the invite because you have similar interests and you're looking to expand your professional network. You can also find these groups on sites like LinkedIn. Search for groups that match what you have to contribute, then check to see which have not just the largest member numbers, but also the most active discussions.

Another way to find your target market online is to investigate competitors' marketing methods. See where another business that offers the same or similar products and services advertises their links and posts on social sites. Be sure each location makes sense and has a large contingent of people in your targeted market. Searching in your field will often turn up places where your audience goes when they're looking for something in your industry.

FYI

If someone is looking for house cleaning services in Orlando, Florida, you should know what they are likely to type into the search engine. You can find out by researching how people search. Good Keywords (goodkeywords.com) offers some great keyword-related software for brainstorming, researching, analyzing, and managing keywords. Free trials are available.

The top social sites to get started with or choose from are LinkedIn, Facebook, Instagram, and Twitter. These sites are massive online communities filled with potential HLNs and TMCs. To get started, set up your profile and navigate to get familiar with the sites' offerings. To stay informed on any social site changes or updates, be sure to bookmark Mashable (mashable. com)—it's one of the leading sources for social networking news and updates.

Groups and Discussions

Even the most introverted entrepreneur can interact on message boards and blogs. Groups and discussion areas on social sites are all over the internet, from LinkedIn and Instagram to Twitter and Facebook. Most social networking sites have community areas for people who have similar interests to gather and connect (even Twitter has groups, or you can join people in discussions around hashtags on a topic—or create your own). It's important to find a dozen or so of these groups and discussion areas and not only join and monitor them, but engage in the conversations as well.

And, as we mentioned earlier, blogs are another type of discussion forum on the internet. A blog isn't just a page on your website; it's a place to interact with your target market. Search for blogs in your fields of interest and leave comments on those that you like.

Blogs are a great way to find HLNs to connect with online, as well as partner with. For example, if you own a restaurant, you could connect with food and review writers, vendors that are blogging, or food enthusiasts, and share their posts and content on your site or blog. This not only builds relationships, but also can expose you to their markets, followers, and fans.

Keep It Separated

It's critically important, in most instances, to keep your personal social media accounts separate from your business accounts. Many people blur the line between professional and personal, but when you own a business, it's more important to be concerned about offending a professional contact with your personal photos or posts. It's best to keep separate Facebook and Twitter accounts, in particular. And if you are a heavy YouTube user, keep your accounts separate there, too.

Facebook Pages

With any social media platform, you need to be creative and find ways to provide value and engage your target market. One of the best ways to accomplish this and position yourself as an industry leader is to build and launch a Facebook page—what used to be called a fan page. If you're an entrepreneur, you can't afford to ignore this powerful tool. People who like and follow a page are enthusiastic, and if they like what they see and read, they'll connect with you, become loyal supporters, and tell their friends.

It's very simple to set up a page for your company on Facebook—just a few clicks, and you're ready to go. You can either create a company page from your homepage on the Facebook site or there are tutorials available in the help section on the site. Once you get your page up and running, pay attention to your analytics, or what Facebook calls "Insights." You can view specific demographic information, such as where your followers are from, their gender, and their age. Monitor who becomes a follower, how they're interacting, and how often they're posting. This will help you figure out who and where else you should be targeting online.

TIP

When looking for groups to join, you'll find many with at least 500 members, which gives you a wide range of people with whom to interact. However, you'll usually find on most social media platforms that a lot of the major groups have only a few members who participate often. Sometimes a smaller group, which fits a niche and is active, can be beneficial as you can get to know one another better. Networking is a numbers game, but sometimes a small number of people can yield bigger results if it is made up of the right people, who understand networking and want to reach out to meet new people.

To enhance the look and brand image of your company page,

use a horizontal image that covers the top of the page invitingly. You should use a smaller logo or image for the inset image that will show up as your page profile photo in follower newsfeeds. You can also set your follower page to have a vanity URL, which is a personalized web name.

One of the main differences between a Facebook profile and a company page is you can send bulk messages to all your followers. You can also "Suggest to Friends" that they join you on your company page. Obviously, this is a feature you need to use wisely, and be careful not to annoy your audience. But it's a great way to connect with your target market, especially because these are connections that have opted-in to become a part of your community. They want to hear from you and talk with you.

"A terrible thing happens without publicity ... nothing!"
—P.T. Barnum

Media Connections on Social Sites

The media is an effective conduit for delivering your messages and story to the people you want to reach and can be vital to gaining word-of-mouth online and off. Most journalists have switched to social media sites because they don't have the time to read lengthy email pitches and press releases. With the help of social networking sites, you can search for media contacts on sites, such as LinkedIn, and reach out to them directly. You can also pitch journalists on Twitter and get up-to-date information about a media outlet and what it's looking for. Look for trending topics in your area or industry and use the prevailing hashtags to get your expertise or product in the conversation when it comes up.

The Troll Equation

Beware of "trolling" (aka trolls) on the net: A troll is someone who posts inflammatory or off-topic messages in an online community, such as a discussion forum, group, or blog, with the primary intent of provoking other users into an emotional response or of otherwise disrupting normal on-topic discussion.

Unless you monitor your blog, social media accounts, etc., there may be no system in place to effectively deal with trolls. This becomes an issue for large platforms like Twitter and Facebook.

What can you do about trolls?

- *Interact.* This means standing up for your company and defending your brand. If someone has something negative to say, but does so in a polite manner, challenge them but do it in a proactive and non-emotional way. This can be hard when you and your company are being attacked, but when you objectively challenge your opponents, much of the time they won't even respond. This will show your happier customers that you've made an effort and potentially ward off further trolling. Trolls don't often think about the fact that there's someone on the other side of that comment because they're used to posting negativity that never gets questioned or tested. When they see that you're paying attention, more often than not, their tones change, the conversation shifts, and you've created a positive interaction.
- *Ignore them.* According to social media management platform, Hootsuite, trolls are there to upset people and cause negative reactions. Don't play their game—and instead, ignore them. Trolls want attention. In some cases, if you refuse to pay attention to them, you deprive them of what they want and they'll go elsewhere. If other people begin to "feed" the troll, you might need to take another tack.
- *Delete.* There are circumstances when it just makes sense to delete the comments. When it's clear that you are not going to be able to get into an effective dialogue with someone, or they've drawn out their trolling buddies, it's time to hit delete.
- *Report.* If a troll is particularly vulgar, disruptive, threatening, or worse, report the social media handle to the platform and follow up until you receive a response. Yelp and some other review sites have a formal complaint process, as do sites like Facebook and Twitter.

Facebook Page Workout

Social media news site Mashable suggests the following tips to enhance and build out your company Facebook page:

- *Twitter integration.* Link your page to Twitter so every time you post, it will automatically be posted to your Twitter account as well. One caveat: If you find your Twitter audience has different interests than your Facebook fans, you might want to consider turning the auto-feed to Twitter off to not alienate those followers.
- *Facebook page blog widget.* Add a widget to your blog to help drive blog traffic and connections to your Facebook page. Facebook provides you with the necessary code.
- *Blog the promotion.* Take your blog to the next level, and link it to your Facebook page.

Start by identifying the media outlets you want to target, and visit the website for each one to research it thoroughly. Keep your list brief so follow-up is manageable. Once you've built your list, search for key contacts at those outlets. LinkedIn is a great resource for finding professional journalists, segment producers, and content managers for other websites. With LinkedIn's search features, you can dive deeper into user data to find contacts that fit your criteria. For example, you can create a search to find contacts with "reporter" as their professional title within a 50-mile radius of your zip code. You can easily narrow each search by limiting other fields or adding a keyword, such as "business" or "features." LinkedIn also lets you save a certain number of searches so you can be alerted to new contacts that join LinkedIn matching your criteria.

Key media contact titles include:

- Editor
- Segment producer

- Journalist
- Reporter
- Assignment desk editor
- Content manager
- Blogger

You can also follow many of these people on their broader social accounts, like Twitter or Instagram, to get a feel for what types of stories they look for and what speaks to the scope of their influence.

Meet the Expert: Stephanie Liu, Video Strategist

Stephanie Liu is a live video strategist for brands and entrepreneurs who want to go from unknown to unforgettable. A digital marketing expert with 15 years of ad agency experience, she has helped thousands of her clients—from moonwalkers to MasterChefs—get on the Fascination Fast Track™ to ignite their ideas and become confident on camera. She is a co-author of the *Ultimate Guide to Social Media Marketing* (Entrepreneur Press, 2020).

How can a small business maximize the power of video to spread the word about their products/services?

Rather than getting lost in the crowd, it's important for businesses like yours to stand out from your competitors. With videos, presenting yourself creatively can quickly convey what your core values are by showcasing how much good work goes into making each product, or providing informational yet entertaining promotional materials on topics such as organic food production methods—all with just one video!

What is the most important factor to consider when planning a video strategy?

The most important factor to consider when planning a video strategy is your mission statement. What type of video content do you plan to make? Whether it's educational, entertaining, or a mix, your brand's expertise and audience needs should determine what kind of approach is taken.

Who are these videos for? Outline the target demographic with as much detail as possible. Think about the buyer personas that would be interested in watching it. You can do this by using a persona template to figure out what they want and need to know. What should your audience take away from your video? A video can be a powerful way to communicate your message and engage with an audience. But it's not just about the content you create, it's also about how you present that content. You want people to take away something from what they watch, so make sure you have a clear idea of what that is before you start filming.

Are there any social video fads/trends that people should avoid?

Jump cuts are a tried-and-true way to edit your footage, but they can also be overused. A jump cut is when the editor cuts out one or more frames in order to speed up time. It's seen as an easy editing technique for new editors because it doesn't require a lot of practice. The problem with this is that too many jump cuts make the viewer feel disconnected from reality, like they're watching a fast-paced video game rather than real life. When you use them sparingly though, they can be very effective at creating suspense and momentum in your story!

Is live video for everyone? How can you know if your audience will respond to it?

Livestreaming for business is an amazing way to not only grow your business, but also connect with potential customers. For our clients, we always do the 10x10 exercise. Make a list of the top ten frequently asked questions that they get about their business, product, or service, and then list the top ten questions that clients should be asking to be better informed. Once they've completed that exercise, they can poll their audience on social to find out which topic viewers are most interested in.

What are some of your favorite live video experiences (short demo, webinar, etc.)?

A well-hosted product demo will allow you to provide prospects with proof that your company's offerings do what they say they will. It'll also give the opportunity for personalization and get them excited about everything you offer!

TIP

The number of PR and marketing people on Twitter is astounding. Use their collective wisdom and networks to create buzz and support for you and/or an event.

Center of Influence List

One of the fastest ways to build referrals and relationships online through social networking is by reconnecting with past friends and family members or simply by reaching out to the top people in your center of influence that respect and admire you. This could be friends from grammar or high school, college, past co-workers, family members, bestselling authors, media contacts, etc.

Media Matters

To find media outlets in your industry or topic area, check out the following sites:

- HARO (Help a Reporter Out) (helpareporter.com) is a free service that connects journalists with expert sources. Each email (there are three a day) includes reporter queries you can respond to (provided you have a relevant pitch or expertise to offer).
- EIN Presswire (einpresswire.com/world-media-directory/) is a regularly updated worldwide listing of TV and radio stations, newspapers/newspaper websites, and blogs.

---

eMarketer.com, a digital marketing and media researcher, reports that more than half (53 percent) of internet users have visited websites referred by friends or family members in the previous 30 days. People trust people that they already know, and your friends and family will most likely recommend you if the situation is right. Referrals have always been an extremely powerful way of gaining customers. With the web, trust levels can be very low for new visitors. In this environment, a referral from a trusted source can make all the difference in converting a contact into a customer.

Develop that trusting relationship with people who are well positioned to help you. You must earn their referrals. When you do, your marketing will become supercharged with what's clearly the best form of advertising—positive word-of-mouth.

Facebook is one of the best sites to connect with friends and family as well as past co-workers and your online center of influence. Once you've determined who these contacts are and connect with them online, you need to not only reach out to them but keep in touch. Have you ever had someone you know buy what you sell from a competitor because they didn't know you sold it? That means you're not at the top of their mind.

Forget Me Not

It is vital that you create a powerful plan to keep your brand top of mind with your contacts. Set aside half a day at least once every three months to reach out to your connections by using one of the following approaches:

- Send them an email once a month. You can announce something new in your business and simply touch base.
- Phone them (or connect via chat or web meeting) to say hello. Ask them how they are first, and keep notes so you have a point of contact for the next call. You can close with an event or big announcement about your company, product, or service.
- Don't tell them, show them how important they are. If this relationship doesn't include reciprocity, it will degenerate into a "what's in it for me?" situation that won't stand the test of time. Send them thank you gifts or online gift cards (a small amount will do just fine) to let them know you're grateful for them and any referrals they've sent your way.

TIP

Twitter is a great site to meet media contacts from around the world.
Once you build a following, try to attend a local tweetup. A tweetup is an
event where people who use Twitter come together to meet in person;
they're great for walking away with a lot of contacts and leads. At a
tweetup, you meet the people you might only otherwise know virtually,
plus the media often attends.

Index

Printed in the USA
CPSIA information can be obtained
at www.ICGtesting.com
JSHW062323280624
65595JS00007B/12